# ACCOUNTING IN SOCIALIST COUNTRIES

# Accounting in Socialist Countries

Edited by
DEREK T. BAILEY

ROUTLEDGE
London and New York

First published in 1988 by
Routledge
11 New Fetter Lane, London EC4P 4EE
Published in the USA by
Routledge
in association with Routledge, Chapman & Hall, Inc.
29 West 35th Street, New York NY 10001

© 1988 D.T. Bailey

Printed in Great Britain by
Billing & Sons Ltd, Worcester

British Library Cataloguing in Publication Data

Accounting in Socialist countries.
  1. Accounting
  I. Bailey, Derek T.
  657
  ISBN 0-415-00429-2

# CONTENTS

## PREFACE

In recent years international accounting has
emerged as a new area of interest to scholars
working at the limits of the expanding frontier of
accounting.
Increasingly the production and commercial
operations of business enterprises span the
boundaries of individual countries. Finance flows
around the globe in search of gainful employment.
The development of the world economy has encouraged
the development of an international perspective on
accounting. The internationalisation of
accounting has become necessary to facilitate the
activities of the transnational corporations and to
facilitate the international flow of capital
seeking profit yielding opportunities. In practice
the term international accounting signifies the
internationalisation of the accounting practices of
the leading capitalist economies as each seeks to
gain an advantage over its rivals in the world
economy. That is, expressed with greater precision,
in the world capitalist economy.
Outside the world capitalist economy there
co-exists the community of socialist countries.
Socialism involves, in one or another form, the
termination of the private ownership of the
principal means of production and natural
resources. Socialism, as Marx indicated, signifies
the end of the reign of capital. The
transformation of the socio-economic institutional
framework consequent upon the changeover from
capitalism to socialism has implications for the
practice of accounting.
The recognition of the international dimension
of accounting has stimulated an interest in the
practice of accounting in socialist countries.
That new-found interest is especially noticeable

Preface

among specialists in Third World countries.
    The purpose of the present book is to fill a
gap in the materials on international accounting by
providing an introduction to accounting in
socialist economies.
    The book in providing a coherent and
systematic approach to its subject matter is
divided into three parts. Part I provides a frame
of reference by reviewing general considerations
affecting accounting in socialist economies. Part
II provides a series of individual studies on
accounting in selected socialist countries. In
Part III there are drawn some general conclusions
that could provide a point of departure for
further   study and research.
    The book is intended to meet a hitherto
unsatisfied need of students attending
undergraduate and postgraduate courses designated
with such titles as 'international accounting' or
'comparative accounting'. The book is intended
also for the increasing number of students who are
choosing to prepare written assignments on
accounting under socialism as part of their
polytechnic or university course of studies. More
generally the book may be of interest to accounting
practitioners and to specialists in the economies
of the socialist countries.
    Thanks are due to accounting specialists in
the GDR, Poland, the USSR and other socialist
countries for the opportunities provided on various
occasions for the discussion of aspects of
accounting under socialism.
    Thanks for their dispassionate but steadfast
encouragement are due to Professor C.W. Nobes of
the University of Reading and to Peter Sowden of
the publishers Routledge.
    Lastly thanks are due to Sue Urquhart.

PART I

SETTING THE SCENE

Chapter One

# INTRODUCTION

Derek Bailey

## The Scope of the Book

Central to the concept of socialism is the principle of the social ownership of the means of production. The term socialism signifies that the use of a society's resources will be socially determined for the generality of society. That is, in a society based on the social, or common, ownership of the means of production the associated producers determine the production and distribution of output through the mechanism of the plan. For the realisation of the socialist objective there is required either the abolition of, or a substantial reduction in, the private ownership of the means of production.

Karl Marx, the outstanding socialist thinker, advanced the argument that behind the formal democracy of the market-place lurked the social relations of capitalism. Under capitalism the labour-power of the workers was exploited necessarily by the private owners of the means of production, the capitalists, who appropriated for their own use a socially generated surplus. Marx argued that under capitalism 'the accumulation of wealth' was accompanied by 'the accumulation of misery' and that the latter was necessary for the functioning of the capitalist economic system. Consequently it was held that the market mechanism of the capitalist system was incapable of satisfying the needs of the greater part of the population. Further, 'the icy water of egotistical calculation', in which the capitalist swam, dissolved social ties and any sense of social responsibilities.

Marx developed his theories during the nineteenth century. At that time great wealth and

acute poverty existed cheek by jowl within the same capitalist economy, as in Victorian England.
Since that time capitalism has expanded to become a world economic system. Today the accumulation of wealth occurs in the advanced industrialised countries and the accumulation of misery occurs in the countries of the Third World.
Under socialism, as generally practised hitherto, economic activities are no longer integrated through the market mechanism acting on the totality of the separate decisions of numerous independent entrepreneurs. Instead, economic activities throughout the country are integrated consciously through the mechanism of state economic planning. As a mechanism of economic integration the market is superseded by the national economic plan. An inevitable consequence is the centralisation of economic decision-making.
The operation of the pricing mechanism is suspended because prices are controlled and fixed by the central authorities. Price ceases to be an indispensable tool signalling essential information to guide entrepreneurs in making decisions on resource allocation. Under socialism such decisions are made by the central authorities on the basis of non-commercial criteria.
Political considerations tend to outweigh economic considerations in the process of decision-making on resource allocation (e.g. the location of new industrial enterprises). The business enterprises cease to be independent and are converted into production units compulsorily required to fulfil the directives on the composition and volume of output issued by the central planning authorities. The management of industrial enterprises loses its commercial dimension and is restricted to a technical dimension. The pursuit of profit is replaced by the quest for higher levels of output. Although the original intention under socialism may have been the satisfaction of needs (e.g. as measured by some kind of social criteria) instead of the satisfaction of demand (i.e. as measured by money in the market-place), the emphasis has come to be placed upon the desirability of a continuously expanding industrial production.
What would happen to accounting with the transition from capitalism to socialism? With the disappearance of the private investor and the privately owned business enterprise would there still be a need for accounting? In the mythology of socialism the accountant has been viewed as the

2

mean-minded henchman of the avaricious capitalist.
With the abolition of private ownership in the
means of production went the abolition of the
paraphernalia of capitalism. Was not accounting,
and specifically double-entry book-keeping, part
of that paraphernalia? Did not its appearance
coincide with the emergence of capitalism? Such
questions have long since ceased to be merely of
theoretical interest.

In the Anglo-American literature accounting
traditionally has been examined in the context of
capitalism. Accounting is conceived as a tool
fashioned to enable the men of business to
prosecute their business affairs with ever greater
success. But socialism implies the repudiation of
those commercial criteria with which the practice
of accounting is impregnated. When a society
undergoes the transformation from capitalism to
socialism, and the means of production are
expropriated from their private owners, may it be
supposed reasonably that accounting will not
remain unaffected? But, how will accounting be
affected?

The purpose of the present book is to attempt
to provide an answer to that question. It does so
by providing an examination of the present state
of accounting in a number of socialist countries.

Immediately there are encountered the problems
of definition and identification. Which countries
are to be deemed to be socialist? A variety of
countries around the world are avowedly socialist.
The concept of socialism becomes increasingly
amorphous the greater the diversity of countries
considered.

For the present purpose a socialist economy is
defined as one in which the principal means of
production, the commanding heights of the economy,
are in public ownership. In such an economy it is
difficult, if not impossible, for some would-be
entrepreneur to acquire a collection of resources
so as to exploit some perceived opportunity for
profit-making. The great majority of the
decisions concerning investment, the composition
and size of the production programmes for
individual branches of industry, and for
individual industrial undertakings, are determined
centrally in the context of a medium term (e.g.
five year) plan for the overall development of the
national economy. In practice the objectives and
priorities incorporated into the national economic
plan are determined by the inner circle (i.e. the

politburo or political committee) of the ruling
political party in what is, in fact if not in law,
a mono-party political process. The ruling
political party adheres to the tenets of Marxism-
Leninism and habitually is referred to as the
communist party although, in fact, it may be
titled differently (e.g. the Socialist Unity Party
in the German Democratic Republic).

By these criteria, and excluding Africa and
Asia generally, the socialist countries comprise:

Union of Soviet Socialist Republics

eight European countries:

| | |
|---|---|
| Albania | Hungary |
| Bulgaria | Poland |
| Czechoslovakia | Rumania |
| German Democratic Republic | Yugoslavia |

one American country:

Cuba

All these countries, with the exception of
Albania and Yugoslavia, are members of the Council
for Mutual Economic Assistance (CMEA), generally
referred to as Comecon.

## The Plan of the Book

The book is divided into three parts. The first
part comprises three chapters and, by way of an
introduction, provides a general consideration of
accounting in socialist countries. The second
part comprises seven chapters of country studies.
In the third part some general conclusions are
drawn.

In the immediately following section of
Chapter I an attempt is made to indicate both the
causes and nature of the major differences between
accounting in socialist countries and capitalist
countries. In the final section of Chapter I
consideration is given to how different models of
the socialist economy may affect the development
of accounting.

In Chapter II there is considered the nature
of the difference between accounting in the
capitalist and socialist countries.

In Chapter III there is outlined the develop-

ment of accounting in the socialist economy.
Each of the seven chapters of the second part
of the book is devoted to a different country.
The countries whose accounting is examined are
Czechoslovakia, Cuba, the German Democratic
Republic, Hungary, Poland, the Union of Soviet
Socialist Republics and Yugoslavia. All these
countries, with the exception of Yugoslavia, may be
characterised as centrally planned economies
although Poland in recent years has introduced a
measure of economic decentralisation and Hungary
has proceeded some distance along the road to
market socialism. In Yugoslavia extensive
economic decentralisation has resulted in the
evolution of a workers' self-managed economic
system (i.e. the director and the managing board
are elected by the workers' council of the
enterprise). Whereas Czechoslovakia and the
German Democractic Republic are advanced
industrial countries, Cuba is a developing country.
The book is a collective work consisting of
contributions provided by:

| | |
|---|---|
| Derek Bailey | lecturer, University of Birmingham, England |
| Wlodzimierz Brzezin | professor of accounting, the Pedagogical University Czestochowa, Poland |
| V.S. Gorelyi | accounting specialist, Havana, Cuba |
| A.V.V. Hercok | late of Mitchell College of Advanced Education, Bathurst, New South Wales, Australia |
| Alicja Jaruga | professor of accounting, University of Lodz, Poland |
| Gerhard Reinecke | professor of accounting, Karl Marx University, Leipzig, German Democratic Republic |
| Rezso Scholcz | head of department, Ministry of Finance, Budapest, Hungary |
| Ivan Turk | professor of management accounting, University of Ljubljana, Yugoslavia |
| Tadeusz Wierzbicki | professor of accounting, University of Szczecin, Poland |

Introduction

Chapter I sections I-III, Chapters II, IX and XI have been provided by D.T. Bailey; Chapter I section IV by T. Wierzbicki; Chapter III jointly by W. Brzezin and A. Jaruga; Chapter IV by V.S. Gorelyi; Chapter V by A.V.V. Hercok; Chapter VI by G. Reinecke; Chapter VII by R. Scholz; Chapter VIII by A. Jaruga and Chapter X by I. Turk.

## Causes and Nature of Differences Between Accounting in Capitalist Countries and Socialist Countries

The practice of accounting is essentially utilitarian, being conditioned by the requirements of the society in which it is conducted. The framework of political and economic institutions of a given society influences the practice of accounting. There is affected both the demands placed upon the accounting function and its process of evolution in responding to changes in those demands. This general statement is equally true both for capitalist countries and for socialist countries. However, there are major differences between the economies of capitalist countries and socialist countries in respect of:

1) the method of ownership of economic resources;

2) the mechanism used in the conduct of economics activities.

Although in many countries there is a combination of public ownership and private ownership of industrial and commercial undertakings, limiting cases are represented by the laissez faire market economy of capitalism and the command economy of socialism. In the former type of economy the economic resources are privately owned. Each entrepreneur independently exercises his own judgement in the conduct of business operations through the mechanism of the market. The entrepreneur acquires resources in those proportions he judges will maximise profits from the subsequent sale of products. In the latter type of economy the economic resources are state-owned. Economic activities are conducted through the planning mechanism. The director of each state enterprise is issued with instructions on the production programme to be fulfilled. He is allocated resources and required to use these to

the best effect in the implementation of the
production programme.  The entrepreneur of the
capitalist enterprise is concerned with the
commercial problem of maintaining the viability of
the enterprise in the market.  The director of the
socialist enterprise in the command economy is
concerned primarily with obtaining technically
feasible solutions to production problems.
        In the laissez faire economy both the volume
and composition of output is affected by
consumers' preferences expressed in the market.
In the command economy output is limited by the
availability of resources.  Abstracting from the
superstructure of legal and political
institutions, the Hungarian economist Kornai has
distinguished between the demand constrained
economy and the resource constrained economy:

> 'An economy is demand constrained if for
> most of the time, the output levels of most
> firms are constrained by demand.
> Conversely, an economy is resource
> constrained if most firms, most of the
> time, are prevented from supplying more
> output by their inability to secure more
> resources, that is, inputs (of either
> labour, materials, or capital).' [1]

        As an initial generalisation, demand
constrained economies may be identified with
capitalism and resource constrained economies,
with socialism.  But, under the severe
difficulties created by a major war the demand
constrained economy of a capitalist country tends
to regress to a resource constrained economy
(e.g. Britain and Germany during World Wars I and
II).  The resource constrained economy can be
effective in the realisation of a limited number
of goals accorded high priority (e.g. as in the
USSR during the period of the early five year
plans).  Generally the resource constrained
economy tends to be less efficient than the demand
constrained economy in the utilisation of
resources.  Consequently, some of the socialist
countries have attempted to move away from a pure
resource constrained economy and, through a
measure of economic decentralisation, create an
'economic mechanism', or surrogate for the market
mechanism, incorporating some of the features of
the demand constrained economy.

socialism

| centralised economies | | | decentralised economies |
|---|---|---|---|
| | command economy (activated by instructions) | 'economic mechanism' (motivated by profit) | |
| | war economy | market economy | |
| | resource constrained economies | demand constrained economies | |

capitalism

The difference in the environment provided by the two types of economy leads to enterprises being guided by different operating rules:

1) demand constrained economy of capitalism - expand profits;

2) resource constrained economy of socialism - expand production.

In the capitalist economy the enterprise is an autonomous decision-making entity. Its survival is dependent upon the maintenance of commercial viability while undertaking a succession of transactions through the market. The entrepreneur is necessarily responsive to price signals concerning factor inputs and product outputs.

In a socialist economy the state enterprise is not an autonomous entity. It is the creation and creature of the central authorities. Usually, losses incurred in the course of fulfilling the production plan will be reimbursed. Unrepaid bank loans will be written off eventually because liquidation of the state enterprise is scarcely even a remote prospect. In the resource constrained economy of socialism:

'... it is the slacks and shortages experienced by individuals firms that provide the signals that influence short-term and long-term adjustment'. [2]

The differences between the demand constrained economy of capitalism and the resource constrained economy of socialism affect the structuring of the accounting system, the scope of the accounting

function, the processing of accounting data, the
use made of data and the role of the accounting
specialist.
   In a capitalist country the government
provides the institutional framework within which
functions the market economy. The government sets
the bounds to permissible business operations
(e.g. by legislation), confines itself to
influencing business behaviour indirectly (e.g. by
fiscal policy) and abstains from direct
intervention in the course of business activities.
There is private ownership of economic resources
and economic activity is conducted through the
market. Investors, both personal and
institutional, provide finance to entrepreneurs
for the acquisition of resources for conversion
into products for subsequent sale on the market.
Investors use the accounting information contained
in corporate reports to guide their decisions on
the purchase and sale of securities and other
investments and the provision of financial
facilities. Entrepreneurs and other business
executives use accounting information to guide
their decisions on resource allocation and to
exercise control over the subsequent conversion of
resource inputs into product outputs. It is for
each businessman to determine for himself how to
arrange and undertake his business activities. He
determines also the nature and extent of the
accounting service needed by the business
enterprise. To satisfy the needs of the
entrepreneur the accounting system evolves in
response to the growing diversity of the
activities undertaken and the increasing
complexity of the internal structure of the
business enterprise.
   The uncertainty inherent in the dynamic market
economy causes the entrepreneur to require a flow
of accounting information so as to monitor the
operating performance and the financial position
of the business undertaking. In addition, the
entrepreneur requires a flow of accounting
information that resolves the choices of economic
action confronting the business into expectations
of revenues, costs and profits so as to guide
decision-making. In the laissez faire economy the
market prices relating to both actual and
prospective transactions provide important
information to the businessman who uses the
accounting service to disclose the consequences of
his actions and to decipher the data provided by

the market.  The accounting practised is
subordinated to the entrepreneur's perception of
his needs (subject to whatever are the current
legislative requirements concerning the keeping of
accounting records and the publication of their
contents).  The accounting entity is set by the
boundaries of the business enterprise.  Although
the execution of the accounting task may be
delegated to a salaried specialist, the
accountant, ultimately it is the entrepreneur who
determines the manner of accounting.

In the capitalist country it is possible for
two identical business undertakings to structure
their accounting data differently from one another
and to provide dissimilar accounting results of
their performance.  Of course, the entrepreneur
and the accounting specialist may not be equally
satisfied with such a situation.  The general body
of accountants, to strengthen their position in
relation to the entrepreneurs may appeal to the
conventions of received accounting practice.  In
the course of time the accountancy profession may
proceed to the enunciation of generally accepted
accounting principles and the formulation of
standards of approved accounting practice.
Nevertheless, it remains a crucial requirement
that these accounting practices are acceptable to
or, at least, are not opposed by the overwhelming
majority of entrepreneurs.

In the socialist country the central
authorities, by means of the national planning
mechanism, determine the activities of each
enterprise.  The socialist enterprise is not
autonomous and, in principle, its corporate plan
is a component of the national economic plan.

State ownership of the industrial enterprises
in the socialist economy leads naturally to the
conception of a common accounting system embracing
all these enterprises.  In effect, the national
economy, or its industrialised segment, becomes
the accounting entity and the individual
enterprise is represented as an accounting
sub-entity.  The accounting system for each and
every enterprise is interconnected through the
implementation of a national chart of accounts.
Thus, the accounting in each and every enterprise
is converted into an instrument of national
economic administration for the realisation of
control over their activities.

In the socialist economy the accounting system
of the enterprise is at the disposal of the

central authorities. In the capitalist economy,
as indicated already, the accounting system is at
the service of the entrepreneur.

In the socialist economy the central
authorities use the accounting system as a means
for maintaining control over the activities of the
state enterprises. In the socialist enterprise
the comptroller, or accountant, is required to
perform a state control function on behalf of the
central authorities. Inevitably, there is tension
between the senior executives of the socialist
enterprise and its accountant. In the capitalist
enterprise the accountant becomes a member of the
management team and tends to absorb its viewpoint.

The operation of the common accounting system
in all socialist enterprises requires the
standardised processing of accounting data. For
its realisation there are required such components
as a national chart of accounts, standard formats
for the accounting records and accounting returns,
authorised accounting procedures and rules for
recording various kinds of transactions.
Accounting procedures are codified and their
implementation buttressed by legal sanctions. The
ministerially authorised accounting regulations in
specifying the obligatory minimum of accounting
procedures are transformed into a part of
administrative law. A specially designated
central authority is responsible for the design,
installation and oversight of the operation of the
national accounting system in each of the
socialist enterprises.

Within the socialist enterprise the planning
function is separated from the accounting function
and entrusted to different officials. The
separation of the two functions, by introducing a
division of responsibilities within the enterprise
may be regarded as a device for strengthening the
ascendancy of the central authorities. For this
purpose it is advantageous to separate a
prospective planning function from a retrospective
accounting function. Two separate communication
channels link the central authorities to the
enterprises: planning directives flowing from the
former to the latter and accounting data on
operating performance flowing in the reverse
direction.

The separation of accounting from planning
permits the coming together of the technical and
economic aspects of decision-making. In general
terms, the socialist enterprise is not confronted

with the commercial problem of deciding what products to be produced with what inputs for sale in which markets so as to obtain the highest profits. Instead, it is confronted with the production problem of determining how best to convert specified material inputs into specified outputs with the given production facilities and manpower. Consequently, the socialist enterprise is orientated to production possibilities and not commercial possibilities. The prime responsibility laid upon the planning department is the operating of the enterprise near the limits of its productive capacity at the lowest cost.

The scope of the accounting function in the socialist enterprise of the command economy is narrower than in the capitalist enterprise operating in the market economy and, in the main, is confined to the operation of the standardised accounting system.

The standardisation and simplification of the work of accounting necessarily decreases the skill required for the exercise of the accounting function and reduces the accounting specialist to the level of competence required by an accounting technician. From the accounting personnel is required the capacity for applying the minutiae of the administrative rules governing the operation of the standardised accounting system. The scope for the exercise of initiative is limited.

In the socialist economy the education and training of accounting personnel comes under state control. For the most part education and training is limited to the provision of a sufficiency of skills for the efficient operation of the standardised accounting system. An undesirable consequence is that the accounting personnel, neither by training nor temperament, are likely to be receptive to any requirement for accounting innovation. More often than not the accounting worker in the socialist economy is a person-ification of the conservative and rule-bound bureaucrat. Both directly and indirectly the standardised accounting system inhibits the modernisation of accounting practice.

In the business enterprise of the capitalist economy the accounting function evolves in response to the changing needs of the entrepreneur operating in the dynamic market economy. A stimulus to the development of accounting practice is ever present.

Generally in the socialist economy there is no

accountancy profession (i.e. an occupational group of self-employed accounting specialists such as public accountants, auditors and tax consultants). An accountancy profession engaged in the provision of a range of accounting and financial services to the business community, so characteristic of the developed capitalist economy, is absent.

Having indicated the causes and nature of the differences between accounting in capitalist countries and socialist countries it is necessary to consider whether the differences are immutable or susceptible to alteration. Before doing so it is desirable to consider more closely the need for accounting information under socialism and to examine accounting in individual socialist countries.

Introduction

## Information Needs and the Development of Accounting in Centrally Planned Economies [3]

Contributed by Tadeusz Wierzbicki

The information system of a centrally planned and directed economy contains three kinds of information:

1) retrospective information — accounting, statistics and techno-operating data;

2) prospective information — plans, prognoses, etc.;

3) reference information — standards, norms, parameters, etc.

Only the accounting system can be regarded as providing comprehensive, authentic and reliable finance and micro-economic information. It is a universal system in that all undertakings are obliged to maintain certain standards of financial and cost accounting in accordance with a uniform accounting plan. Accounting, as a source for central statistics, delivers aggregated information to the central authorities for the managing of the national economy.

The role of accounting as an information system is determined by the demand from management for information. At the macro level (i.e. the entire national economy) this demand is determined by three main factors:

1) the degree of development of the forces of production;

2) the complexity of relationships in the economy;

3) the degree of decentralisation in decision-making.

The third factor is dependent on the general model applied in the management of the national economy.

At the macro level management is required to ensure that all organs within the national economy (undertakings, concerns, etc.) perform the centrally planned tasks. It can be achieved in one of three ways by adopting:

14

1) the command model - undertakings received 'from above' precise tasks to be performed with prescribed and limited resources in conditions of highly centralised decision-making;

2) the parametric model - undertakings are influenced by economic instruments (prices, taxes, wages, etc.) and synoptic measures (profit, added value) to attain an economically optimum performance of the central plan (itself established as a result of a significant degree of decentralisation in decision-making);

3) mixed model - containing elements of both the command and the parametric models.

A modern developed economy, if centrally planned and directed, exhibits a relatively low demand for accounting information. The significant decisions are made only at the central level and are issued as directives to the peripheral organs. Through a system of statements and reports the central authorities specify the information to be provided by the peripheral organs. The potentially rich sources of accounting information are insufficiently utilised by:

(1) the undertaking where:

(a) the information flows are designed primarily for the satisfaction of the information needs of the central organs and not those of the undertaking's management

(b) the economic information made available by these information flows is superfluous to the needs of the undertaking's management because of the small scope for decision-making;

(2) the central organs where:

(a) the accounts are compiled mainly in non-monetary units (i.e. physical quantities)

(b)  the financial data, although readily
available, is utilised in only a
few macro-accounts - national
income, balance of payments, income
and expenditure balance of the
population.

The command model for the management of the
national economy does not encourage the
development of the information function of
accounting and leads to a decline in accounting.
Practical confirmation is to be found in such
facts as:

1)  the relatively low application of modern
computing techniques;

2)  the loosening of the links between
financial accounting (i.e. the ledger
control accounts) and the analytical
accounts (i.e. the subsidiary accounts
for stock, wages, etc.) when
computerisation does occur;

3)  a decline in the prestige of accounting as
an information source for management;

4)  the underdevelopment of macro-accounting
applications:

a)  the absence of national economic
accounting

b)  the imperfections of accounting theory
and practice at the interface of
micro- and macro-information (i.e. in
the design of financial statements)

c)  the under-appreciation of balance and
value methods in macro-statistics and
central planning;

5)  the difficult situation in the accountancy
profession, such as lack of qualified
staff, comparatively low salaries, uneven
and slow organisational and technical
progress, etc.

The contraction in the information function of
accounting is irreversible without a radical
change in the nature of the demand for

information.   That demand will not change while a command model is used for the direction of the national economy.

For the improvement of accounting, as well as for society generally, much interest is presented by the attempts at economic decentralisation and the application of economic instruments for the indirect steering of the national economy (i.e. with the transition from a command model to a parametric model for national economic management). At the beginning of the decade in Poland the first steps were taken through the partial introduction of a new economic and financial system.  In strengthening the role of central planning the new system replaces the obligatory directives by indirect instruments, such as prices, taxes, bank interest, etc.

The new financial and economic system is expected to stimulate a demand for management information tailored to the needs of the low and middle ranks of the managerial hierarchy and especially to lead to:

- the expansion of information concerning costs, income, stocks and funds;

- the automatisation of operational analysis;

- the simulation of plan variants;

and simultaneously to:

- the elimination of superfluous information;

- the restriction of the vertical information flow;

- the enlargement of the horizontal information flow (concerning customers, markets, etc.).

The central organs for planning and management will require additional detailed information concerning the behaviour of undertakings in the context of the new economic and financial system (e.g. to improve the steering parameters).

The changes in the Polish economic system provide a great opportunity for the development of accounting in the centrally planned economy by utilising the latest advances in management accounting and cost accounting, and, at the central level, in national accounting with the aid of modern data processing techniques and methods.

## REFERENCES

1. Hare, P.G., Economics of Shortage and Non-Price Control, Journal of Comparative Economics, Vol.6, 1982, p.408.
2. Op. cit., p.409.
3. An edited extract of a paper originally presented in March 1980 at the Third Congress of the European Accounting Association in Amsterdam.

Chapter Two

## THE BUSINESS OF ACCOUNTING: EAST AND WEST

Derek Bailey

## Introduction

An acquaintance with Soviet accounting literature
reveals that the glavnyi bukhgalter, the chief
accountant to the Soviet enterprise, is occupied
mostly with routine data processing tasks. A
closer acquaintance with Soviet society reveals
that accounting is an occupation lacking in status
and prestige and that, unlike the advanced
industrial societies of North America and Western
Europe, the accountants have not emerged as a
major profession. The unusual fact that the
second industrial power in the world lacks an
influencial and prestigious accounting profession
requires an explanation, the more so as the
extension of the use of accounting has been
associated with economic development. [1] In this
Chapter an attempt is made to furnish some answers
to this question. It is suggested that the answer
may reside in the differences between the economic
environment, the institutional framework of the
market economy and the planned economy, although
such factors as historical experience and the
nature of accounting itself may not be without
significance.

## Integrating Economic Activities

The integration of economic activities at the
micro-level in any economy may be achieved in one
of three principal ways. That is by integration
through market transaction, by administration or
by cooperation. The first involves contractual
agreement between independent and freely
negotiating parties, although interlocking

directorates may be an important factor in
achieving such agreements.  The second includes
the administration of the economic activities
within a firm by its management.  Also included is
the administration of legally independent firms by
ministerial directive, as in the management of the
British war economy 1940-45, and administration by
planning.  The third includes not only cooperative
undertakings but also joint venture activities.
An example is Polygram, the sound recordings group,
jointly owned by NV Philips' Goeilampenfabrieken
and Siemens A.G.

Integration through market transaction or by
administration are not mutually exclusive
categories, most economies comprising a judicious
although changing admixture of the two methods.
In Britain, since the Coal Nationalisation Act
1946, economic integration of the coal-mining
industry has been realised through the exercise of
administrative powers by a state corporation but
the coordination of the industry's activities with
other parts of the economy has been realised
through market transactions.  Real-world economies
may be visualised as being located at different
points in a continuum extending from a pure case
of integration by market transactions to one of
integration by administration.  As a
generalisation, and so far as manufacturing
industry is concerned, Britain and the U.S.S.R.
fall towards opposite ends of the continuum,
although the crucial economic difference between
the two societies is the method of ownership of
the means of production: private and state,
respectively.  Integration through the market,
with private ownership of the means of production,
requires its own set of institutions and actors:
capital markets, commodity exchanges, financiers,
stockbrokers and entrepreneurs.  The state planned
economy requires planning organs and planners.
Are there any grounds for supposing that, whereas
accountants are habitués of the market economy,
the planned economy gets by with
engineering-economists and bookkeepers?


## Soviet Economy

The politburo of the Communist Party of the Soviet
Union, in conjunction with the Council of
Ministers, determines the key decisions on the
division of output between investment and

consumption, composition of the investment programme, innovation, rate and direction of industrial expansion. These decisions are influenced by previous economic achievements, estimation of unrealised potential of installed productive capacity, the external and internal political situation, and represent the priorities to be observed by the central planners when drawing up the national economic plan.

The national plan is drafted in terms of physical quantities of inputs and outputs. The state planning mechanism attempts to integrate economic transactions, and to determine both resource allocation and income distribution across the national economy. Through a succession of closer approximations projected supply and demand are brought into equilibrium. After the state planners have attempted the planned coordination of the economic activities for the major sectors of the economy the national plan is disaggregated to the various industrial ministries and thence to enterprises. Economic decision-making on behalf of the enterprises is centralised, the large decisions of where, what and how much to produce being taken by the state planners. The implementation of such decisions is delegated to individual enterprises. The directors of enterprises are not empowered with entrepreneurial responsibility and it is probably more accurate to say that the directors administer, rather than manage, the enterprise.

When the basic planning has been completed in real magnitudes the plans are recalculated in monetary values by multiplying the planned quantities by prices. The prices of resource inputs - materials, basic wage rates, finance - and of commodity outputs are decided by the state planning organs. Prices are utilised as devices of accounting control and, as a general rule, are not used as decision criteria. Monetary values provide a common unit of aggregation, a check on internal consistency and are needed for the compilation of cash, credit and investment financing plans. The conversion of the plans from physical quantities into monetary values is needed to permit:

1) exercise of financial control over the enterprises;

2) assessment of the performance of various enterprises on a comparable basis;

3) calculation of the enterprise's cost of output;

during the currency of the plan.

Accounting, in the sense of data processing, provides a convenient mechanism for monitoring the flow of resources and commodity outputs and for exercising financial control over the enterprise. Such surveillance, conducted through the state banking network and other organisations is intended to ensure that the activities of enterprises are directed towards the implementation of the goals assigned by the central planners. All receipts and payments on behalf of enterprises must be channelled through the State Bank, which receives and scrutinises copies of the authorising paperwork and is empowered to block irregular movement of funds. The controls are not directed to ensuring the commercial viability of the enterprise's operations.

The enterprise is confronted with a schedule of authorised prices for factor inputs and commodity outputs, an allocation of materials and a permitted level of manpower employment. On the basis of the assigned goals the enterprise plans, in effect schedules, production for their efficient realisation within the limits of the materials allocation and manpower availability. The problems encountered include machine manning and loading, the determination of production mix, size and sequence of production batches. The enterprises need to attract and retain workers through the promise of bonus earnings and superior fringe benefits made possible by the efficient management of the production process. In doing so it is necessary to achieve the stipulated targets for commodity output deliveries (e.g. units of footwear dispatched to and accepted by the distribution network). Variations in the rate of turnover quantities for different selling lines within the product range may be met by appropriate adjustments in the production programme. But, given the enterprise has no control over prices, its behavioural response is more likely to be conditioned by considerations of profitability (and, hence, of the effect on future bonus earnings) than by the desire to meet consumer preferences.

The rehabilitation of the 'profit motive'
during the mid-sixties signified a recognition of
the importance of monetary incentives for
efficient plan management and the motivation to
work. Profit has been harnessed to production and
not business purposes, to the improvement of
production efficiency and not the conquest of
markets. Enterprises are expected to produce
saleable commodities but not to 'pander to
consumerism' in quest of profits. The Soviet
enterprise does not have a business problem
because it is not burdened with maintaining its
commercial viability. In consequence enterprise
managements' attention is dominated by the
production problem, which is primarily a technical
problem although it has economic implications.
Against a setting of pre-determined prices and
outputs profit is designed to be a generalised
measure of successful (production) plan fulfilment.


## Accounting in the Soviet Economy

In a planned economy, such as the U.S.S.R., the
enterprise functions within an environment
structured by the state. Because the enterprise
operates to satisfy the goals assigned by the
state planners and the demands of the market, the
directors are not clothed with entrepreneurial
responsibility. Strategic planning is not within
the area of competence of enterprise management.
The directors are not confronted with problems of
commercial viability; that is, with maintaining
sufficient liquidity, profitability and sales
orders to ensure the survival of the enterprise.
The business decision-making powers of the
enterprise directors, stemming from the 1965
Economic Reform, are delegated and discretionary
and, unlike the powers of their counterparts in
the market economy, are not omnipresent and
mandatory. The enterprise director has a reduced
need for accounting information and the role of
the accounting function is altered.

The accounting tasks performed for the firm in
the market economy, and anticipated to be required
for the Soviet enterprise, are concerned with
economy rationality, planning and control.
Because of differences in the modus operandi,
these tasks are distributed among various
specialists to meet the specific requirements of

the planned economy. The content of the tasks undergoes alteration as follows:

1) The application of economic rationality to the selection of goals. The objective may be described as the maximisation of production, rather than profit, and the task is performed by the central planners.

2) Enterprise planning. Because the goals have been determined by the central planners the task remaining is the scheduling of production, determining the utilisation of equipment and manpower so as to maximise labour productivity. The planning goals are incorporated into a production programme. Specialists with skills in the technology and economics of manufacturing are needed. These are the chief economist and the subordinated planning workers at the enterprise.

3) Enterprise control. It comprises the accounting mechanism for monitoring the execution of the plan and the accomplishment of the planning goals. The control over planning at enterprise level is performed by the chief bookkeeper.

Whereas (1) and (2) above are concerned with prospective activities and involve data analysis, (3) relates to current operations and requires data processing. Comparing the dramatis personae of the business firm and the Soviet enterprise, instead of:

(a) the accountant advising management on the basis of accounting information - a bookkeeper;

(b) the business economist deals with problems of diversification into new products, technologies and markets and acts as an engineering-economist.

The demarcation between accounting and engineering economy obtaining in the Soviet enterprise corresponds to that drawn in a different context by Thuessen and Fabrycky: [2]

'The accounting system of an enterprise
provides a medium for recording historical
data arising from the essential
activities employed in the production of
goods and services.  Engineering economy
analysis provides a means for quantifying the
expected future differences in the work and
cost of alternative engineering proposals.
As compared with this function, accounting
has the objective of providing summaries of
the status of an enterprise in terms of
assets and liabilities so that the condition
of the enterprise may be judged at any point
in time.'

Some writers continue, 'Accounting
records are one of the most important sources
of data for engineering economy studies ...
In addition, the outcome of decisions based
on economy studies will eventually be
revealed in these records.' [3]

Coincidentally, it is the distinction between
the roles of accounting and engineering economy
drawn by these two writers that is to be observed
in the Soviet enterprise in the distribution of
duties between the chief bookkeeper and the chief
economist.  Although coincidental, such a
distribution presumably reflects the dominance of
engineers, and not businessmen, in the management
of the Soviet enterprise.

'The term engineering economy may be defined
as a body of knowledge, techniques and
practices of analysis and synthesis involving
an attitude toward human factors useful in
evaluating the worth of physical products and
services in relation to their cost.  The noun
economy means management with thrift.  This
meaning, coupled with the term engineering,
embodies the idea of maximum service per unit
of cost, through engineering.  The primary
function of engineering economy analysis is
the quantitative evaluation of engineering
proposals, in terms of worth and cost before
they are undertaken.' [4]

The respective tasks of engineering economy
and accounting are summed in the Soviet terms
'regime of economy' and 'rouble control'.  'The
regime of economy ... consists in saving ...

25

working time, materials and money.' [5]  'Rouble
control is carried out by keeping accounts of its
input and output and comparing them in money
terms.' [6]
       Because the integration of economic activities
is undertaken by the state, by administrative
means, and not by each individual enterprise
through market transactions, the state replaces
the enterprise as the prime user of accounting
data. Accounting acquires a macro- instead of a
micro-orientation.  The prime requirements of
accounting for state purposes are:

    1)  safeguarding property in the possession of
        enterprises;

    2)  ensuring such property is used only for
        designated purposes;

    3)  capability for summarising data to provide
        a condensed view of the aggregate
        activities of enterprises by region,
        industry and for the entire country;

    4)  scope for analysis of the overall results
        of enterprise and industry operations.

Hence, the primary consideration is the fulfilment
of a control function.  Secondly, providing an
overview rather than a detailed analysis of
enterprise operation.  To this end (1) a
standardised accounting system providing an output
of periodical accounting returns to the
supervising agencies is needed and (2)
bukhgalterskii uchet is separated from operativnyi
uchet.
       Double entry bookkeeping is concerned
primarily as a device for classifying accounting
data, whether it or some alternative
classification device be employed is a matter of
convenience in assembling data prior to its
transmission to the supervising authorities.
Accounting is employed as a wholly backward
looking and not forward looking tool.  Accounting
is but one of a number of controls over the
enterprise and which reinforce one another.  In
these circumstances, where there is both
integration by administration and standardised
accounting, the accountant is superseded by an
accounting technician, the glavnyi bukhalter,
fulfilling the tasks of bookkeeping and

26

internal audit.

Some of these tendencies are to be observed in advanced private enterprise economies.

'Accounting data constitute one of the richest sources of economic statistics. The effective operation of a "mixed" economy, regulated largely by prices and profits, is dependent upon information accumulated in the accounting system and ancillary records of business enterprises. Without the various returns utilising these data made by businesses, the numerous government agencies, the whole machinery of economic control of the economy as we know it would be greatly impaired, in some cases rendered impossible.' [7]

## Market Economy

The directors of private enterprise firms in the market economy are concerned with such problems as the acquisition and mix of factor inputs, the determination of the products and services to be supplied to which markets under what conditions. And also with problems of the conversion of factor inputs into outputs, the choice of production technology and its utilisation. Because firms are important centres of economic power the solution of these problems requires an ongoing process of negotiation leading to the creation of mutual contractual obligations integrating the activities of the firm with other parts of the economy through a succession of market transactions. The exercise of entrepreneurial responsibility, which the process involves, stems from the firm's independent existence, its survival being dependent upon achieving and maintaining a level of profitability sufficient to enable the firm to ride out the consequences of inept decision-making and fluctuations in the level of business activity. Recognition of, and receptivity to new opportunities for making profits is an important attribute of business management in the market economy. The economic facts-of-life of the market economy necessarily constrain the directors when reviewing a range of alternative business strategies.

Because the private enterprise firm is an autonomous decision-making entity, albeit that the

27

bounds within  which the directors may act of their
own volition are steadily drawn tighter by
increasing state intervention, there exists the
business problem of ensuring the commercial
viability of the business: deciding what to do and
how it is to be done so as to yield a profit.
Subordinated to the business problem is the
production problem of making the most effective
use of a production plant equipped with specific
facilities.  The subordinate position of the
production problem is evidenced by the degree of
idle productivity capacity possessed by firms. The
business problem is centred upon the improvement
of economic efficiency.  The production problem
resolves itself into the choice of the most
efficient means to obtain a given production and
is primarily a matter of technical efficiency,
although there is an economic aspect.

       With economic decision-making and the
concomitant exercise of economic power
decentralised to individual firms uncertainty is
ever present in, and generated by the manner of
functioning of the market economy. [8]  The
increased scale of business activities, of
production plant capacity as well as the size of
firms, the increased proportion of costs
unavoidable in the short-run and the gestation
period for, and the longevity of the effects of
business decisions causes the directors to become
increasingly dependent upon an input of
information to inform and guide their
decision-making deliberations. There has arisen
the concept of an accounting information service
responsive to the changing needs of management as
it reacts to changes in the market environment.

       The quickening pace of technological change,
product obsolescence, and shifts in market demand
heighten the importance of the entrepreneurial
over the managerial aspect of business direction
and control.  Entrepreneurial ability is the flair
for recognising and the skill in responding to new,
unexploited  profit making opportunities and may
be distinguished from the managerial ability
applied to the implementation of entrepreneurial
propositions and to the administration of current
business operations.  Again, there is an increased
demand for an input of information.

       Confronted with uncertainty the directors of
the smaller market dominated firm tend to be
guided by the operational rule that, unless
demonstrably false, the immediate future will not

be very different from the immediate past. The
smaller firm requires an input of information
concerning the immediate past to aid the efficient
functioning of the decision-making process. The
larger firm dominates the market and through the
internal planning system of its technostructure
influences the nature of its environment. To do
so there is required an input of information to
both the entrepreneurial function and the planning
system of its technostructure. [9]

## Accounting in the Market Economy

The rise to prominence of the accountant is
attributable to the need to delegate additional
powers and responsibilities with the increasing
size and scale of business operations. The sole
entrepreneur was able to oversee all the
activities of the business and arrive at decisions
on the basis of a personal awareness of the
opportunities facing the firm. With the
development of industry and commerce there emerged
the corporate business undertaking and, within it,
the entrepreneurial function serviced by a corps
of specialist advisers. During the same time the
accountant emerged from the chrysalis stage of
counting-house clerk and was transformed from one
who merely 'kept the books' into the adviser to
the directors on the financial implications of
current activities and contemplated actions. By
retaining control of the bookkeeping system the
accountant became concerned with both the
processing and analysis of data expressed in
monetary terms. The accountant's duties included
the advisory and control functions and money
management. The control function is carried out
with the aid of the older techniques of double-
entry bookkeeping and the new techniques of
budgetary control and standard costing. Because
of the dynamic interaction between the firm and
its market environment the advisory function is
not restricted to, or primarily devoted to
production activities occurring within the firm.
The accountant's advisory function is primarily
upon the firm being impelled to maintain its
commercial viability by means of a continuous
stream of appropriate market transactions.
'Economists sum up the integrating process that
markets perform by saying that market prices
allocate resources among alternative output uses,

and wage, rent and interest incomes among the
resource owners.' [10]  'The economic categories
of wages, profit, interest on capital, etc. ...
express quite well the viable relations of the
capitalist system and as such they have pragmatic
utility, being of service in management and the
taking of decisions ...' [11]  These are the kinds
of categories utilised by the accountant.  Used,
for example, when constructing a set of budgets for
profit planning purposes or evaluating a proposed
diversification strategy. The money management
function is intimately connected with the
commercial viability imperative, being concerned
with the acquisition and disposition of monetary
resources and embracing debtors' and creditors'
control and securities management.

The two factors of (1) the crucial role of the
accountant as the guardian of the firm's solvency
and (2) the versatility of  the tool of double-
entry bookkeeping, whether as a data classifying
device, or as a means for establishing methods of
control or for constructing financial models of
the firm, have provided a solid foundation upon
which accountants have built up a position of
considerable influence in industry and commerce.
This occurs where the firm (1) exists as an
independent decision-making entity; (2) interacts
with other firms and institutions through market
transactions; and (3) is faced with the
uncertainty inherent in the market economy.

Other factors have assisted the growth of the
accounting profession.  In Britain, for example,
both professional opportunism and the methods of
training have contributed.  The accountant has
grown in stature through appropriating from other
specialists those responsibilities whose
successful exercise required inter alia a
knowledge of accounting.  From the later years of
the nineteenth century accountants, rather than
lawyers, have become the principal experts in the
field of taxation practice.  The accounting
profession has acquired expertise in such areas as
executorship, trusts, portfolio management,
bankruptcy, company liquidations, reconstructions
and mergers.  From around the years of the First
World War accountants superseded engineers as
costing specialists. During the 1920s and '30s,
when contracting markets threatened the solvency
and survival of firms, and problems of liquidity
and not administration dominated the thought of
directors, the accountant tended to replace the

company secretary as the directors' senior
adviser. In more recent times the accountant has
come gradually to assume responsibility for the
utilisation of business computer systems and such
newer areas of managerial professionalism as
operational research, corporate planning and
taxation planning have tended to be encompassed.
These developments are a testimony to the pivotal
position in the managerial hierarchy
held by accountants and to the significance of
their contribution to succcessful business
operation for firms in the market economy.
　　For the prospective accountant the serving of
time in a capacity akin to that of an apprentice
ensures that he acquires a sure grasp of the basic
accounting routines. He acquires the competence,
should necessity so require, to take on the tasks
of payroll preparation of bought ledger reconcilia-
tion. The accountant has the practical skills
personally to intervene and release potentially
damaging blocks in the firm's cash flow.
　　A number of tasks that have come within the
purview of the accounting function have arisen
through the development of advanced industrial
societies. These societies are characterised by
state intervention in business affairs. Such
intervention is normally clothed in legislative
form. The demise of the laissez faire economy, in
which there is minimal state intervention in the
management of business enterprise, and the rise of
the state-managed economy has been accompanied by
an increasingly voluminous, complex and rapidly
changing legislation affecting the costs and
revenues of business. A widening range of taxes,
subsidies, levies, grants, incentives and, more
recently, prices and wages controls bear upon the
viability of business and the manner of business
operation and have served to enlarge the role and
enhance the status of the accountant.
Increasingly accountants are recruited into
directorial positions.

## The Accounting Field

A delineation of the accounting field may be
attempted in terms of work content (i.e. what is
accounting?) or role performance (i.e. what do
accountants do?).

'Some people naively confuse a bookkeeper
with an accountant and bookkeeping with
accounting.  In effect they confuse one of
the minor parts with the whole of
accounting...  Bookkeeping is the routine and
clerical side of accounting and requires only
minimal knowledge of the accounting model.  A
bookkeeper records the repetitive and
uncomplicated transactions in most businesses
and may maintain the simple records of a very
small business.  In contrast, the accountant
is a professional who is competent in systems
design, analysis of complex economic events,
interpretative and analytical processes,
financial advising and managerial
endeavours.' [12]

This confusion reflects a change in the
accountant's perception of his own role. nearly
three-quarters of a century earlier the accountant
had been more narrowly defined as 'one who is
competent to design and control the system of
accounts required to record the immense volume of
transactions that take place every day in the
world of industry, trade and finance', [13] a
definition that corresponds more closely to that
of a head bookkeeper and implies an exclusive
concern with the bookkeeping system.  For the
purposes of this Chapter accounting, conjoined with
the contiguous field of finance, may be said to
comprise data processing and data analysis, the
data utilised being expressed in a common monetary
unit (and thereby is distinguished from, say,
technical, medical or other sorts of data).
Data processing may be subdivided into:

I   (a) financial accounting - to record
        market transactions and, arising
        therefrom, relations with other
        parties;

    (b) cost accounting  - to record the
        conversion of resource factors into
        outputs.

Data analysis may be subdivided into:

II  (a) financial analysis - data analysis to
        assist financial management decision-
        making;

(b) cost analysis - data analysis to assist product management decision-making.

Askew to the above neat classification the accounting field may be dissected to reveal additionally:

III (a) management accounting - design installation and operation of accounting control techniques;

(b) accounts analysis - data analysis to assist the evaluation of past performance.

Whereas I(a) and II(a) are concerned with the integration through the market by means of current and prospective transactions, I(b) and II(b) are directed to accounting work arising from the integration of current and prospective operations within the firm. In relation to the time scale, I(a) and I(b) concern antecedent, and II(a) and II(b) prospective transactions and operations. Finally, III(a) and III(b) deal with past and more closely current external market transactions and internal conversion operations.

With the transformation of a market economy into a planned economy involving the nationalisation of the means of production, integration of economic activities by administration, loss of entrepreneurial responsibility by enterprises and consequential simplification of legislation (e.g. taxation law) the content of accounting work is reduced. A sizeable part of the know-how of the accountant is contingent upon serving the needs of senior managements attempting to integrate the economic activities of individual firms through market transactions. In the U.S.S.R. integration is centralised and undertaken by such organisations as the State Planning Commission and the State Bank. Features drawn from financial and cost accounting were incorporated into the standardised accounting system devised by the Ministry of Finance in conjunction with the Central Statistical Administration and applied in all enterprises throughout the Soviet Union. The implementation of the successive modifications to, and refinements in the system, and its smooth

33

functioning generally was, until 1960, a major
preoccupation of accounting workers. The
institutional and structural changes that occurred
in the U.S.S.R. reduced further the work of
accountants. Money management on behalf of the
enterprise and accounts analysis, the evaluation
of an enterprise's performance from the accounting
returns, became the responsibility, if not the
prerogative, of the State Bank. In the
centralised planning economy, with the enterprise
responding to directives issued by the state
planners, financial analysis and cost analysis
were not developed as accounting tools. Redundancy
in the accounts know-how, the loss of tasks to
other institutions and the atrophy of other tasks
caused the accounting field to contract to data
gathering and processing conducted in conformity
with the standardised accounting system.
'Accounting as a classification and measurement
system can be operated, understood and used by
folks at the high school level.' [14] The Soviet
accounting system demanded, and demands, the
ability to keep abreast of, and to adhere to the
regulations and rules issued by the Ministry of
Finance and other state authorities. The residual
legatees of the accounting profession are the
glavnye bukhgaltery employed on data processing
and occupying positions comparable to those of
accounting technicians.
     The development of the standardised accounting
system ensured that scarce skilled manpower would
not be absorbed by the accounting function of
enterprises. Accounting skills are exercised by
other actors in the planned economy.

Within the enterprise:

chief economist - accounting and technical
data analysis for production scheduling and
improving production efficiency.

Beyond the enterprise:

state bankers      - money management for the
                     enterprise
                   - accounts analysis

state auditors     - audit and inspection of
                     accounting personnel and
                     procedures

systems designers - design of data processing
and reporting systems

industrial ministry officials - accounts
analysis

The pool of skilled personnel engaged on the
more exacting tasks of systems design and audit
are under the central control of various
ministries and other state organs.

During the era of the command economy (roughly
1930-60) the enterprise was wholly the creature of
the central planners and approximated to a
production unit rather than a business
undertaking. The central planners specified the
production programme, operating losses were met
out of the State Budget and there would appear to
have been little incentive for undertaking data
analysis. With the introduction of the Economic
Reform in the mid-1960s, enterprises were
empowered to prepare their own production
programmes around a set of planning targets
assigned by the state planners. These low-skilled
accounting technicians, the glavnye bukhgaltery,
were not suited generally to the more exacting
task of cost analysis for advising enterprise
management. This task has tended to fall to the
chief economist although the failure to develop in
earlier years comprehensive costing procedures and
techniques probably acted as a brake on the
success of the measures of economic reform.

In answer to the question: 'what has become of the
persons who could reasonably be expected to have
been absorbed into the accounting profession of an
advanced industrial country?' it may be suggested
that in the U.S.S.R. such persons became
economists preoccupied with tackling the planning
problem encountered in various state agencies.


Accounting in History

The nature of the accounting function changes
according to the stage of socio-economic evolution
and the institutional framework of different
societies, and is schematically illustrated in
Table I.

Table I

| Social structure | Feudal | Capitalist | Socialist |
|---|---|---|---|
| Form of accounting | Charge and discharge | Double entry | |
| | | Individual | Standardised |
| Function | Data processing | Data processing and data analysis | Data processing |
| Purpose | Control | Control and planning | Control |

Traditionally, the accountant has been occupied with maintaining an historical record in monetary terms of the activities of institutions and undertakings and with the protection of specie, paper money, valuables and other assets. Down the centuries the accountant has passed successively through the guises of steward to the feudal estate, counting-house clerk or bookkeeper to the business venture of early capitalism and accountant to the firm of advanced industrial capitalism.

In feudal society the major task confronting accounting was the establishment of personal accountability: holding a person to account for the collection and dispersion of specific funds in the course of their duties. With the development of capitalism, accounting was needed to improve the survival prospects of the nascent business undertakings, liquidity rather than profitability being the prime concern. Accounting records were important aids to the entrepreneur in maintaining commercial viability. Ensuring sufficient liquidity to enable the business to survive was a major preoccupation in an age when the consequences of bankruptcy could be horrendous. Under industrial capitalism, expenditure control came to be a major consideration leading to the development of budgeting and, latterly, to the concept of control through programme budgeting. There may be observed a progressive evolution and extension of data processing techniques and the uses to which they may be harnessed.

Emerging as a by-product of data processing, but gaining in importance with the increasing

scale and complexity of business operations and
the quickening pace of changes in the market
environment (e.g. innovation in technologies and
products, shifts in patterns of demand, changes in
governmental policies and in overseas markets),
data analysis for advising the firm's directors on
the financial implications of contemplated
business strategies emerged as an important part
of the expanding accounting function.  The
enlargement of the accounting function is
dependent upon the firm being a major centre of
economic decision-making power.  This
characteristic feature of the market economy
disappears with the transformation into a planned
economy.  The locus of economic decision-making
power shifts from a multitude of micro-units of
economic activity to the central state agencies.
There is a contraction in the scope of the
accounting function and the need for accountants.
In the U.S.S.R. the 'accountant' regresses to
exercising solely a control function, as in
pre-capitalist society.  He is concerned with
personal accountability, expenditure control and
the monitoring of the progress towards the
realisation of the plan's goals.  In some measure,
to the formative influences of specific features
particular to the Soviet Union may be attributed
the role acquired by accounting in that country.


## Historical Influences

There were a number of historical factors
influencing the development of Soviet accounting.
The Italian or double-entry bookkeeping was not
introduced into Russia until the later decades of
the eighteenth century, some 240 years after its
first appearance in England.  But its use spread
slowly and by the early decades of the twentieth
century there was no established accounting press,
no professional grouping of accountants.  In the
large foreign-owned firms accounting seems to have
been handled by expatriates.  Those accounting
workers who remained in the country following the
October Revolution of 1917 refused to cooperate
with the new Soviet regime and during the 1920s
may well have been deterred from so doing by the
sporadic outbursts of 'spetz baiting', the
castigating as 'politically unreliable'
specialists of bourgeois origin.  The state-owned
enterprises fell under the domination of Party

members and engineers, persons who were either ideologically or professionally and, frequently, on both grounds, antipathetic to an accountant's preoccupation with financial considerations, which considerations receded further into the background during the industrialisation drive of the first and second Five Year Plans (1928-37). During the decades extending from 1930 to 1970 accounting workers in the U.S.S.R. were quarantined from acquiring an appreciation of the improvement in accounting techniques occurring in the advanced industrial countries. In particular, the Soviet accounting workers were immune from the influence of the development transforming the scope and content of accounting in U.S.A. and Britain during the post 1945 period. From this time and, until the Economic Reform announced in 1965, khozraschet, or economic accountability, bore a 'formal character' [15] in the Soviet Union. Efforts were concentrated on improving bookkeeping systems and the accounting role did not progress beyond data processing, the prime function of accounting being the continuous recording of the enterprise's activities and the cyclical submission of a series of accounting returns to various state authorities.

Conclusion

Would it have been possible for Soviet accounting to have undertaken data analysis with the aim of furnishing an input of information to the decision-making process as has occurred in the business firm of the market economy? If not at enterprise level, then at state level?

Using accounting data for planning purposes is, in the absence of other information, based on an extrapolation of current trends. Accounting data is a dependent variable and is socially conditioned. The value judgements implied in the accounting data would have reflected the structure of costs of the status quo and, at the time of the Stalinist industrialisation drive, would have been inimical to the powerful political forces intent upon a thorough-going transformation of Russian society. The purpose of the Stalinist industrialisation drive was to bring about a decisive and radical change in the economic and social infrastructure. In these conditions accounting data could not be used as a guide to action. Stalin's dictum of industrialise or be vanquished could not be reduced to an accounting formula usable as an operational rule. The Stalinist industrialisation drive may be characterised 'as a result of animal spirits - of a spontaneous urge to action, rather than inaction, and not as the outcome of a weighted average of quantitative benefits multiplied by quantitative probabilies'. [16] Of a comparable tempestuous upheaval Pollard observed that 'entrepreneurialship in the industrial revolution did not develop to any significant extent the use of accounts in guiding management decisions'. [17] Accounting adapted itself to the practices of businesmen. But commercially minded (i.e. market orientated and profit motivated) businessmen were absent from the U.S.S.R.

It seems reasonable then to infer that the pre-eminent position of the accountant as an adviser to the heads of firms or enterprises is not inherent in the institutional framework of every advanced industrial society. 'We cannot change one variable without affecting all the others', [18] Hill remarked of the transition from feudalism to capitalism in Britain. An observation which is likewise true of the transition from capitalism to socialism. With the disappearance of the autonomous business firm the raison d'etre of the accountant qua accountant also vanished.

NOTES

1. Published in Journal of Management Studies, Vol.12, No.1, 1975, pp.28-44 and reproduced with permission.

REFERENCES

1. 'Enterprise accounting promises great potential for assisting the economic development of developing nations.' See Scott, G.M., Accounting and Developing Nations, Washington: University of Washington Press 1970, p.1.
2. Thuessen, H.G. and Fabrycky, W.J., Engineering Economy, Englewood Cliffs, N.J.: Prentice-Hall, 1950, p.349.
3. Ibid.
4. Ibid., p.8.
5. Institute of Economics of the Academy of Sciences of the U.S.S.R., Political Economy, London: Lawrence and Wishart, 1957, p.615.
6. Ibid., p.621.
7. Amey, L.R. and Egginton, D.A., Management Accounting - A Conceptual Approach, London: Longman, 1973, p.13.
8. Robinson, J. and Eatwell, J., An Introduction to Modern Economics, London: McGraw-Hill, 1973.
9. Galbraith, J.K., Economics and the Public Purpose, London: Andre Deutsch, 1974, analyses the private enterprise economy into the two sub-systems called 'market system' and 'planning system' within each of which the firms are respectively environment-determined and environment determining.
10. Dalton, G., Economic Systems and Society, London: Penguin, 1974, p.37.
11. Godelier, M., Rationality and Irrationality in Economics, London: NLB, 1972, p.xxv.
12. Welsch, G.A. and Anthony, R.N., Fundamentals of Financial Accounting, Homewood, Illinois: 1974, p.18.
13. Lighthand, R.M., 'The Present and Future of the Accountancy Profession', The Accountant, 4 December 1920, p.605.
14. Devine, C.B., 'A Critique', in Burns, T.J. (Ed.), The Behavioral Aspects of Accounting Data for Performance Evaluation, Cleveland, Ohio: Ohio Stte University Press, 1970, p.287.
15. Harasik, M.A. and Siginevich, A.V., Financy i Khozraschet v Promyshlennosti, Lenizdat, 1973, p.29.
16. Keynes, N.M., The General Theory of Employment, Interest and Money, London: Macmillan, 1960, p.161.
17. Pollard, S., The Genesis of Modern Management, London: Penguin Books, 1968, p.289.
18. Hill, C., Reformation to Industrial Revolution, London: Penguin Books, 1969, p.16.

Chapter Three

## ACCOUNTING EVOLUTION IN A PLANNED ECONOMY

W. Brzezin and Alicja Jaruga

## Introduction

As is generally known, accounting, and in
particular double-entry bookkeeping, was described
by Pacioli some 500 years ago as a set of methods
to portray in monetary terms the economic reality
of micro-business transactions. Changes in the
contemporary world have, however, necessitated
considerable changes in accounting practice and
theory.
   The development of accounting practice is
affected also by the increasing use of accounting
information for managerial and control purposes as
well as by the rapid development of computers.
   In the twentieth century, accounting policy in
a number of countries was reflected in the legal
regulation of accounting practice. Complete
unification was reflected in the elaboration of
uniform charts of accounts (in the 1930s) and in
the establishment of uniform accounting in
centrally planned countries.
   Accounting theory has been extended to cover
such developments in accounting practice.
   New problems emerged in the field of
accounting when the socialist economy was
developed. Socialist countries adopted the basic
apparatus: ledger accounts, the double-entry
principle, and the balance sheet. However, the
attributes of an economy which is centrally
planned and based on a unique pattern of property
ownership created both new organisational problems
as well as those connected with the merits of
accounting itself. Hitherto the solution of
problems has proved the basic principles of
accounting to be universal and the source of new

experiences which could be further generalised.
In our opinion, the modern theory of accounting
should generalise experience both in micro- and
macro-accounting and should be broad enough to
provide bases for accounting practices both in
socialist and capitalist countries.

A consideration of the problems of accounting
development in a centrally-planned economy,
(taking as examples the U.S.S.R., Poland and to a
lesser extent, the GDR) could throw new light on
the theory of accounting.

It would be easier to understand accounting in
the Soviet Union by making a rough survey of
accounting development in that country at the
start of the twentieth century. Briefly
summarised, four phases in the development of
accounting in the Soviet Union and the European
socialist countries may be distinguished:

1) 1917 to 1930, when conventional accounting was
   used in Soviet Russia to meet the needs of
   business practice

2) 1930 to 1945, marked the development of
   individual and non-conventional recording
   solutions adapted to the need for control of
   the economic processes covered by the national
   economic plans (first 5-year plans)

3) 1945 to 1956, was the period when Soviet
   accounting directly influenced the development
   of uniform accounting in other socialist
   countries

4) the period after 1956 when each socialist
   country developed its own accounting system.

## Short Review of Accounting in Russia at the Start of the Twentieth Century

The start of the twentieth century is a
particularly important period in the history of
accounting in Russia. [1] A great demand for
qualified accountants emerged in this period of
time. At first special courses were organised for
the education of specialists in accounting and
then higher education in economics and allied
studies commenced. Institutes of Higher Commercial
Studies were created in Moscow in 1906, in Kiev
in 1907 and in Petersburg in 1915 [2] and brought

about growing concern with the development of
accounting theory.  In 1888 the magazine
'Schetovodstvo' was first issued and very soon
established close links with the European
accounting thought through its publication  of
articles devoted to the theories of G. Cerboni,
L. Gomberg, J.F. Schar and many other authors.
        Very talented teachers of accounting such as
J.J. Sivers, N.S. Lunskii, N.A. Blatov, A.P.
Rudanovskii and others made great contributions to
the development of accounting theory in Russia at
the turn of the 19th century.  Most of these
authors developed their theories of accounting
after the Revolution in Russia by searching for
new solutions relevant to the requirements of the
centrally planned economy.
        A.P. Rudanovskii played a very important role
in the development of Russian accounting theory.
In 1912 he published a book on double-entry bookkeeping theory incorporating elements of
mathematics. In the opinion of the Soviet accounting historian, V.A. Mazdarov this book represented
a great achievement not only in Russian but also
in world literature. [3] The elaboration of macro-
economic theory of a balance sheet is considered
to be the greatest achievement of A.P. Rudanovskii
[4] although it belongs to the post-Revolution
period in Soviet accounting history.  B.L. Isajev,
a modern specialist, in his works often refers to
the statements made by Rudanovskii in his
monograph on macro-economic theory of a balance
sheet. [5]
        B.L. Isajev's opinion is that the national
economic balance sheets developed by A.P.
Rudanovskii have not yet been applied in the
Soviet Union.  In its day, A.P. Rudanovskii's work
was far ahead of the theory of social accounting
in West European countries.
        J.F. Walicki is another author who played a
very special role in the development of Russian
accounting theory.  His work [6] was the first
attempt in world literature to apply accounting to
macro-economic needs.  On the basis of research
made in Moscow and Leningrad libraries [7] it has
been established that in January 1898 Franciszek
Ksawery Walicki lived in Petersburg and was a
barrister.  He died on the 2nd of January 1898 and
was buried in the Roman Catholic cemetery and
there is a plate on his tomb bearing the
inscription in Polish.  Thus it may be concluded
that J.F. Walicki was either a Russian scientist

of Polish origin or a Pole writing in Russian during the period of the Polish partition.

Walicki's approach, unknown hitherto in world literature deserves recognition and attention. In his view, social capital consists of various items which should be expressed in monetary terms. Thanks to valuation in monetary units those items can be classified as follows: [8]

$$a, b, c, \ldots \qquad j, k$$

The total of those items (resources) will represent, according to Walicki, the value of national wealth:

$$a + b + c + \ldots \qquad + j + k = S \qquad (1)$$

The left-hand side of the equation represents components and the total of assets whereas the right-hand side stands for owner's equity plus liabilities. Owner's equity stands for social capital (S) and liabilities represent foreign debts (D). Thus the extended shape of balance sheets could be expressed as below:

$$a + b + c + \ldots \qquad + j + k = S + D \qquad (2)$$

Any increase of assets on a macro-level results from the growth in volume of production of various goods and this can be illustrated as follows: [9]

$$\alpha, \beta, \psi \ldots \qquad \gamma, \tau = P \qquad (3)$$

The left-hand side of the equation stands for goods manufactured, the right-hand side aggregates all products being manufactured.

Any decrease of national assets results from the consumption process (C) and could be illustrated as below:

$$u + t + v + \ldots \qquad + n + q = C \qquad (4)$$

The left-hand side of the equation stands for goods consumed and the right-hand side for total consumption. The difference between P and C will thus represent the balance that has not been consumed and is equal to the growth of social capital (S).

Based on equations (2), (3) and (4), Walicki has developed an extended balance-sheet equation:

44

$$(a + \alpha - u) + (b + \beta - t) + (c + \psi - v) +$$

$$\ldots \qquad + (j + \gamma - n) +$$

$$(k + \tau - q) = S + (P - C) + D \qquad (5)$$

The above equation represents a simplified description of the changes in national wealth. The most illuminating elements of Walicki's theory lie in bringing wealth into relationship with production, consumption and accumulation processes. For the first time in that stage of development of macro-balance sheet theory, foreign debts (liabilities) were introduced. Thus, Walicki was the first in world literature to prove that accounting is able to describe economic realities of macro-economic entities.

Even on the basis of such fragmentary information about the development of Russian accounting theory it could be stated that the Russian accounting theorists made a considerable contribution to the development of the world's theory of accounting.

## Accounting in the Soviet Union 1917-1930

Organisational problems of accounting were well appreciated from the very first years of the Soviet state. To a great degree it was thanks to V.I. Lenin who, in his writings and speeches, considered accounting to be a necessary requirement for central control of the national economy. Nowadays it could be represented by a cybernetic approach as illustrated on the following page.

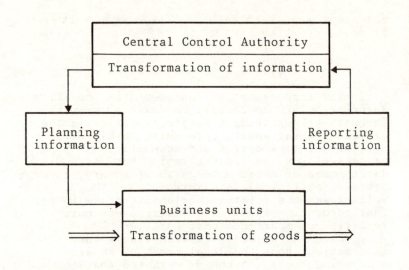

Diagram 1

Accounting, as a custodial function, should
and could be applied in all state-owned
enterprises and institutions as well as in
co-operatives.

The development of accounting practices
required highly qualified accountants, and
educational programmes were based both on domestic
and foreign accounting literature.  In the period
from 1917 to 1930 accounting in the Soviet Union
was based on principles similar to those in
capitalist enterprises.  However, as new financial
systems and categories appeared there arose a need
to redesign the accounting systems.

## Accounting in the Soviet Union in 1930 - 1956

In the nineteen thirties the financial system was
reformed in the Soviet Union.  A consequence of
the reform was that the greater part of enterprise
profit came to be profit appropriated by the
Government Budget. [10] This period generated both
theoretical [11] and practical approaches to
accounting. [12]  These could be considered as
original concepts with respect to adjusting
accounting to the needs of a centrally planned
socialist economy.  Very strong intervention by

the government with respect to the principles and
practice of accounting could be noticed in this
period in the Soviet Union. Accounting was
oriented mainly to monitoring the implementation
of production plans, having rigidly prescribed
inputs and outputs. At this same period the
titles of accounts as well as detailed procedures
recording were made uniform. The number of
accounts in the general ledger was considerably
increased to 120 items. Uniform financial
statements were also introduced. The Soviet chart
of accounts for industrial enterprises, developed
in 1940, could be considered as another important
achievement of this period. The chart of accounts
reflected the evolution of detailed bookkeeping
pinciples in that both the names of the account
and the recording principles were precisely laid
down. Thus it could be said that totally uniform
accounting at that time was created.

[Soviet accounting influenced to a considerable
extent the approaches to accounting followed in
other socialist countries such as Poland, the GDR,
Czechoslovakia, etc. The new charts of accounts
that emerged in those countries after 1950 were
closely designed upon the Soviet model. [13] After
1956, the charts of accounts in individual
socialist countries were adjusted to accord with
their particular financial systems, and to provide
for the incentives (premium and bonuses) system
related to the improvement of business performance.]

## Development of Accounting in Poland After 1944

After World War II, accounting in Poland was based
on a uniform chart of accounts introduced in 1946
and based on the German charts of accounts used
during the war. The chart of accounts was
reformed in 1950 and only then were new elements
introduced. The new chart created a separate
recording system for fixed assets and investments,
the latter being considered very narrowly as an
equivalent to an increase in fixed assets. The
new chart of accounts introduced in 1953 was based
on the Soviet approach to the keeping of
accounting records.

Only the succeeding reform of the chart of
accounts which took place in 1960 contained a new
approach to accounting to correspond with the
changes in planning and management of the Polish
national economy. The new approach was intended

to evaluate the performance of relatively autonomous business units and not only disclose conformity with legal regulations and formal budgeting. [14]

## Accounting and Financial System in a Socialist Economy

Accounting is closely connected to the financial system of enterprises. In a socialist economy finance appears through the commodity - money relations arising in the conduct of economic activities. The gross national product and national income are reflected in financial flows. Finance embraces the entire economic phenomena affecting the generation, and utilisation of national income or, in other words, concerning the accumulation and allocation of financial resources. [15]
    In a socialist economy the financial system, adapted to the system of national economic management, is determined by the central state authorities. Under the system of direct management of the national economy the state budget plays a major role in the financing of economic activity. Under the system of indirect management of the national economy, bank loans occupy a major place in the financing of the operations of business enterprises.
    The financial system in the socialist economy embraces the following area:

- financial system of enterprises
- State Budget
- banking system
- insurance system
- utilisation of public funds
- international finance.

    All the above areas together form an organic whole and through the process of distribution of the national income are disclosed the inter-relations that exist in the total financial system.
    The simplified model of how the financial system works in a socialist economy could be illustrated on the following page:

### Financial System in a Socialist Economy

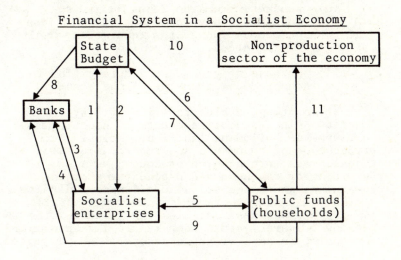

Diagram 2

where:

1) payments from enterprises to the State Budget

2) transfers from the State Budget to enterprises

3) bank loans raised by enterprises

4) loans repayment, bank interest, bank charges related to clearing transactions

5) public revenues and expenditures (households)

6) revenues (salaries) of those employed in a non-production sector of the economy

7) payments from the public to the State Budget (taxes)

8) cash transfers (from the State Budget) designed to finance investment

9) bank loans (short-term and for consumption purposes) provided and repaid savings deposited by households

10) transfers from the State Budget to
finance the development of the
non-production sector (education, health
service etc.)

11) purchase of goods and services from the
non-production sector of the economy.

Accounting enables the financial system to
function. In a socialist economy accounting
services the following functions exclusively:
preparation of documents and recording of clearing
transactions, preparation of documents and
recording of revenues and expenditures of the
government and all institutions financed directly
by the State Budget, recording national assets
assigned to business entities and recording the
persons (cashier, store-keeper, etc.) responsible
for a certain part of those assets.

## Micro- and Macro-Economic Aspects of Accounting

In a socialist system, accounting by its nature,
serves micro- and macro-economic purposes. As
stated above, Walicki and then Rudanovskii were
the first to recognise the macro-economic
functions of accounting. Their ideas, however,
have not been used in the process of establishing
socio-economic accounting systems. Enterprise
accounting remained at the micro-economic level,
although accounting information generated at the
enterprise level was and is used to draw up macro-
balance-sheets. Accounting methods help to
consolidate financial reporting only at the level
of unions of enterprises (equivalent to concerns)
whereas consolidation of data on the level of
ministries and on the level of the Council of
Ministers is made through statistical records.
The consolidation of financial statements at
the central level of the economy is made difficult
by the existing charts of accounts and because the
uniform basic economic and financial terminology
is used in day-to-day planning and bookkeeping and
the uniform principles of financial reporting, are
orientated towards micro-entities.
The successful application of the double-entry
principle to social accounting focused the
attention of Polish and Russian theorists on the
possibilities of using this princple for macro-
planning and macro-recording purposes. Then the

idea of integrated micro- and macro-accounting was born. Tadeusz Peche [16] is considered to have originated the idea in Poland. Attention was focused on the construction of charts of accounts from the macro-accounting viewpoint but there is a long way, unfortunately, to its full application. [17]

The concept of charts of accounts has proved to be very useful, but twenty years have passed from its emergence in 1911 to its final implementation. It is most likely that the concept of integrated micro- and macro-accounting will be slow to be applied. In the Soviet Union statisticians above all appreciate the need for the implementation of this concept. The works of B.L. Isajev [18] on the scope for the application of social accounting in the USSR strongly emphasise the need for micro- and macro-accounting integration.

The idea of integrated micro- and macro-accounting has already been applied in the GDR. In 1966, the East German authorities stated that for planning and management purposes statistics should be integrated with accounting into one information system able to serve the needs of both enterprise management and the central management of the national economy. In that same year they introduced the Uniform Accounting and Statistics System. The new system is likely to satisfy the information needs of the national economy better than do any of the accounting information systems in other socialist countries.

Enterprise accounting constitutes a recording system based on documents, however it is limited to information expressed in monetary units, whereas statistics not applied in this systematic way, are not always based on documents and yet supply a much broader range of qualitative information. The integration of accounting and elements of statistics should facilitate the better adjustment of economic information to management needs. It may be suspected, however, that accounting functions will tend to be taken over by statistical departments when the scope of decisions made at the enterprise level decreases. At present one can notice an opposite tendency, however.

## Accounting and the National Economic Management System

The role of accounting in a socialist economy changes not only with the socio-economic development of the country but is also affected by the system for the planning and management of the national economy applied in a given country during a specified period. Generally, there can be distinguished the direct model and the indirect model. [19]

Under the direct management system economic information conveyed from the centre to enterprises is of a directive nature. In such a situation business performance can be measured in physical units and prices are used for aggregation only and fulfil a passive function. In the direct management model the role of statistical information increases and the functions of accounting are limited.

Under a decentralised, indirect management system economic information conveyed from the centre to enterprises is of a motivational nature. The information is conveyed through economic variables, such as: price, rate of return on assets, interest rate on bank loans, and other parameters and regulators.

The role of accounting expands when the indirect system of economic management is applied. The performance of enterprises can be evaluated not only by quantitative measures (e.g. volume of production) but also, if not primarily, by efficiency measures such as the level of plan implementation expressed in profit or value added. Accounting information becomes necessary for operational management and for the evaluation of the performance of senior executives in the effective utilisation of resources.

In the nineteen-sixties and nineteen-seventies decentralised economic systems combined with central strategic planning were introduced in all socialist countries. Accounting is required to supply comprehensive information on the performance efficiency of enterprises. There is a tendency to combine the enterprises into larger organisations. This tendency is noticeable in all socialist countries.

In the Soviet Union business organisations cover associations of enterprises under a particular Ministry [20] (e.g. Ministry of Electronic Devices). In Bulgaria business

(economic) complexes have been created, whereas in
the GDR there exist branch (vertical) and
territorial (horizontal) business organisations
(plants) which are operated as reproduction
(investment) centres.  In Poland big business
organisations have been established covering all
branches of industry and construction. These
organisations work on the basis of full economic
accountability.  The state form of ownership [21]
has created a collective economy in which there
exists no stock market.  State-owned enterprises
operate on an economic accountability basis and a
decentralised administration of enterprises'
resources aims at the achievement of National
Economic Plan targets.  The implementation of the
central plans is ensured and the individual
motivation (incentives) system works efficiently.
The motivation system is based on the principle of
workers' participation in planning and control
processes as well as on their participation in
allocation of the surplus.  The main task of
management accounting is to distinguish the  non-
controllable variables and to filter their impact
on the financial results of different
responsibility (accountability) centres: cost,
profit (value added) and investment centres.

## Special Features of Accounting in a Centrally Planned Economy

Accounting is completely uniform in this economy.
The uniform chart of accounts, financial
statements and assets' valuation are based on the
principles, standards and rules of accounting.
Economic, administration and financial law
regulations also have a strong impact on
accounting.  Hence custodianship and stewardship
are the main accounting functions.  The system of
supplying data for efficiency control is mainly
determined by financial standards as well as by
planning principles and regulations i.e. it rather
evaluates events (facts) from the viewpoint of
their potential rationality (according to the
rule) reflected in a set of regulations. [22]
Standardised accounting typically is regarded as a
system of evidence that enables control to be
based on documents of a highly objective nature.
        Accounting theory is based mainly on the
Marxist theory of economy.  For example:
enterprises are not subject to market exchange
because there is only one (state) form of

proprietorship; Land is not considered a commodity and thus is not subject to valuation (excluding private farming).

Enterprises are not profit orientated. They are operated as sub-entities and integral parts of the whole society. Therefore accounting provides reports on the contribution the particular organisations make to the entire society. Accounting helps the centrally planned and systematically controlled economy work.

Valuation standards are based on historic cost. Periodical and occasional changes in the prices of materials and finished goods are made exclusively by the state authorities. The adjustment of the valuation of fixed assets takes place less frequently. The last revaluation of fixed assets occurred in 1962. The prices for imported raw materials are frequently stabilised so as to maintain price stability for goods in the domestic market. [23]

Financial accounting and cost accounting (management accounting) are integrated and interdependent. The same applies to micro- and macro-accounting.

Uniform accounting in Poland covers:

- uniform chart of accounts (see Diagram 3),

- model charts of accounts and accounting guidelines for each branch of industry,

- uniform financial statements (terminology, codification and presentation).

The main financial statements are:

- Balance Sheet in which groups of assets are compared with the appropriate sources of financing in order to evaluate whether financial rules are followed by a particular enterprise (see Diagram 4),

- Comparative Income Statement used for macro-accounting purposes and showing:

  - costs by nature
  - revenues by nature

- Profit and Loss (Net Income) Account showing:

- balance of trading account (profit or loss)
- extraordinary items of expenses and revenues.

- <u>Income Distribution Statement</u>

- <u>Funds Flow Statement</u>

- <u>Social Activities Statement</u>.

Cost determination is based generally on full (absorption) costing. In many industries standard costing and flexible budgeting is applied. For special decisions the marginal approach is used mainly in Hungary and Poland. Based on standard costs (conversion costs) averaged for a particular branch of industry so called initial prices are set up for products. These prices are used as a cost basis for selling price formation. To assist central planning factors of production, new multi-task (multi-purpose) cost accounting models are being designed. These models emphasise the utilisation of resources through different phases of a product life-cycle. [24]

<u>UNIFORM CHART OF ACCOUNTS</u>
since 1976 (groups)

0  Fixed Assets
1  Cash and Bank Loans
2  Receivables, Payables and Claims
3  Inventories - Materials
4  Costs by Nature
5  Costs for Allocation and Losses
6  Finished Goods Inventories
7  Revenues and Income
8  Basic Funds and Financial Results
9  Funds for Special Purposes and Central Budget

<u>Diagram 3</u>

## BALANCE SHEET STRUCTURE

| ASSETS | FUNDS and LIABILITIES |
|---|---|
| Investment operations | Investment funds, investment bank loans, and payables |
| Fixed and detached | Statutory fund for fixed assets |
| Inventories and prepayments | Statutory fund for current assets |
| | Short-term bank loans |
| Receivables from customers | Payables to suppliers |
| Cash and other receivables | Other payables |
| Profit allocated | Financial result (profit) |
| Assets for special purpose activities | Funds and liabilities of special purpose activities |

Diagram 4

## REFERENCES

1. Brzezin W., S problematyki powstania i rozwoju radzieckich planow kont (On Creation and Development of Soviet Charts of Accounts), Acta Universitatis Copernici, Torun, 1978.
2. Mazdarov, V.A., Istorija rozvitija buhgaltierskogo utschota v SSSR (History of Bookkeeping Development in the USSR), Moscow 1972 p.18.
3. Mazdarov, V.A., ibidem, p.38.
4. Rudanovskii, A.P., Postrojenije gosudarstviennogo balansa (Creation of National Economy Balance-sheet), Moscow 1928.
5. Isajev, B.L., Balansi miezotrasljevih finansovih svjazej (Balance-sheets of Inter-branch Financial Links), Moscow, 1973, pp.17-23;
   Isajev, B.L., Integrirovannije balansovije sistiemy v analizie i planirovanii ekonomiki (Integrated Balance-sheet Systems and Economic Analysis and Planning), Moscow, 1969.
6. Walicki, J.F., Teoria stchetovodstva v primienienii k narodnomu hozjajstvu s prilozienijem sostojanija stchotov po ekonomii Rosiji (Book-keeping Theory and National Economy - Russian case), S. Petersburg, 1877.
7. Letters of 18.7.1972 No.23/2/86 from V.I. Lenin Library in Moscow to S.G. Pis. Library in Warsaw;
   Letter of 18.8.1976 No.4772/76 MK from M.E. Soltykov-Stchedrin Library in Leningrad to the Nicolaus Copernicus University Library in Torun.
8. Walicki, J.F., ibidem, p.1.
9. Walicki, J.F., ibidem, p.2.
10. Mazdarov, V.A., ibidem.
11. Strumilin, S.G., K pierestrojkie buhgaltierskogo utschota (Towards Reform of Book-keeping), Moscow, 1934.
12. Nikolajev, M.V., Buhgaltierskij utschot i obschtschije voporsy organizacji utschota, (Book-keeping and General Problems of its Organisation), Moscow, 1934.
13. Brzezin, W., Polskie plany kont w swietle teorii rachunkowosci (Polish Charts of Accounts and Accounting Theory), Ph.D. dissertation, Warsaw, 1969;
   see also: J. Blecha, Der Tschechoslowachische kontenrahmen fur Industriebeliebe und die Organisation ihres Rechnungswesens, Zeitschrift fur Betriebswirtschaftslehre, No.5/1962;

see also: A.A. Jaruga, Problems of Uniform Accounting Principles in Poland, The International Journal of Accounting, vol.8, No.1, 1972, The University of Illinois, 1972, pp.25-42.

14. Jaruga, A.A., Some Developments of Auditing in Poland, The International Journal of Accounting, vol.12, No.1, 1976, pp.101-109;
✓ see also: A.A. Jaruga, The Accountancy Profession in a Centrally Planned Economy: the Polish case, The Accountant's Magazine, Scotland, October, 1979, pp.428-430.

15. Bosiakjaski, Z., Polityka ekonomiczna (Economic Policy), SGPIS, Warsaw, 1976, p.191.

16. Peche, T., Rachunkowoscprza dsiebiorstw a rachunkowosc spoleczna (Enterprise Accounting and Social Accounting), Warsaw 1959; and Podstawy wspolczesnej ewidencji gospodarczej (Fundamentals of Current Economic Recording), Warsaw 1973, 1976.

17. For details see: A.A. Jaruga, Workers' Self government and Reporting: New Dimensions of Accounting Systems in Poland, Brussels, 1979.

18. Isajev, B.L., Balansi miezotraslejevih finansovih svjazej (Balance-sheets of Inter-branch Financial Links), Moscow, 1973; and Integrirovannije balangovije sistiemy v analize i planirovanii ekonomiki (Integrated Balance-sheet Systems and Economic Analysis and Planning), Moscow, 1969.

19. Trzeciakowski, W., Indirect Management in a Centrally Planned Economy, North-Holland Pub. Co., Amsterdam, 1978, pp.9-38.

20. Jaruga, A.A., and Z. Jaglinska, Further Developments of the Economic System in the USSR, Soviet Accounting Bulletin, Vol.VII, No.3, Autumn 1979, University of Birmingham.

21. Agriculture (ca. 80 per cent of land belongs to individual farmers) and handicraft are exceptions to the rule.

22. For more details see: A.A. Jaruga, The Nature of Accounting in Poland, Congress of the European Accounting Association, Paris, 1978.

23. For more details see: J. Gorski, and A.A. Jaruga, Theoretical and Practical Problems of Accounting for Changing Prices in Poland, in: The Impact of Inflation on Accounting. A Global View, The International Journal of Accounting, University of Illinois, 1979, pp.88-102.

24. For more details see: A.A. Jaruga, and J. Skowronski, Multi-goal Cost Accounting Model and EPD System, Systems Analysis Applications to Complex Programs, Pergamon Press, London, 1978.

PART II

COUNTRY STUDIES

Chapter Four

**ACCOUNTING IN CUBA**

V.S. Gorelyi

An Introduction

In realisation of the decisions of the First
Congress of the Communist Party of Cuba there was
a radical reconstruction of the entire  system of
management of the economy on the basis of the
utlisation of the basic elements of the modern
economic mechanism, the forms and methods of
management for a socialist society and the
experience acquired by socialist countries.
In Cuba much attention was given to the
development and introduction of a new system of
planning and management of the economy, including
the organisation of accounting and reporting.
After the Cuban Revolution the system of
accounting and reporting information was adapted
to changes in the forms and methods of planning
and management in the various stages of
development of the economy. In recent years the
'economic register' accounting system functioned
in conditions marked by the absence of
commodity-money relations, the principles of
economic accountability, financial and credit
relations of the enterprise with the State Budget,
and the bank, etc.  The system was used for the
collection and summarisation of the authorised
range of national and equivalent value indicators
for subsequent statistical processing. In these
circumstances neither the form of organisation nor
the methods of accounting were able to satisfy the
new demand of planning and management for a
systematic reflection of the results of economic
and financial activities of enterprises, for their
generalisation in value terms and for the
implementation of the control, analytical and

other functions inherent in accounting.

A large group of Cuban scholars and accounting specialists prepared materials for the basic regulations on the national system of accounting and reporting. These were examined by a Commission for the development and introduction of the new system of planning and management, approved in July 1976, and issued in the form of special instructions: accounting in enterprises and accounting for budgetary activities. The instructions disclosed the accounts chart, the features of the first order and second order accounts and directions for their application, the model correspondence of accounts, the schedule of the principal primary documents and accounting registers for the synthetic and analytical accounts, model balance sheets and other reporting forms and also the principles of organisation of production accounting, expenditure accounting and product cost determination.

On 1 January 1977 the new system of accounting and reporting came into operation in all state enterprises and budgetary institutions. The basic regulations for the accounting system stipulated:

1.  a unified accounts chart for economic operations (for economic accountability and budgetary activities) consisting of nine divisions or groups of synthetic accounts and sub-accounts:

    100 basic means and other non-circulating assets

    200 normed circulating means

    300 monetary means and other means in exchange

    400 owned and equivalent sources of financing

    500 bank credits against normal circulating means and reserves

    600 other credits and financing

    700 revenues

    800 expenditures

    900 results

The initial variant of the plan contained 77
control accounts and 48 sub-accounts; 25
control accounts were designated for the
economic operations of both enterprises and
budgetary institutions; 6 accounts for
budgetary activities only and the remainder
for only economic accountability activities.

2.  separate systems of accounting reports for
    enterprises and economic organisations and for
    budgetary institutions.  The first group
    includes the overall balance sheet (unified
    for all types of economic activities), profits
    and losses reports, cost of realised commodity
    output, cost of realised commodities (for
    trading activities), summary of expenditure by
    economic elements, report on capital
    expenditure, movement on the state capital
    investment fund (or State Fund).  The reports
    for the budgetary institutions included the
    overall balance sheet reports, reports on the
    implementation of the expenditure estimate,
    analyses of expenditure by sub-headings and
    expense items, reports of current expenditure.
    Reports are presented quarterly and annually.
    In 1978 the compilation of a monthly balance
    sheet was recommended in experimental
    enterprises transferred to full economic
    accountability.

3.  the overall principles of production
    expenditure accounting and product cost
    determination, specifying the grouping of
    expenditures by so-called 'cost centres' and
    the calculation of the cost of a unit of
    output.  Because of the difficulties
    encountered in this section of the planning
    and accounting work there was created a
    special commission comprising representatives
    of the State Planning Commission, the State
    Committees for Finance, Prices and Statistics,
    the National Bank and also the economic
    services of the leading branch ministries for
    the direction of the preparation of the Basic
    Regulations for Planning, Accounting and
    Product Cost Determination.

    The majority of enterprises apply the
journal-ledger (or American) form of accounting
and in some instances it has been adapted to
mechanisation with the aid of keyboard calculating

machines. Several enterprises have experience of
the utilisation of punched card accounting
machines and computers. For important sections of
accounting (basic means of production, labour and
wages, material values and commodities, account
settlement and payment operations, etc.) model
forms of primary accounting documents have been
recommended to enterprises and institutions.
However, there is much work to be done in
regulating the system of primary documentation.

The methodological guidance of accounting and
reporting and the conduct of measures for the
introduction and improvement of the new accounting
system has been entrusted to the State Committee
for Finance. These functions are performed by the
Committee's National Accounting System
Administration which includes the following
departments:

general methodology of accounting

organisation of accounting in industry and
trade

organisation of accounting in agriculture,
construction, transport and other activities

organisation of accounting in budgetary
institutions

mechanisation and centralisation of accounting.

Questions related to the development of a
system of primary accounting documentation are
dealt with by the State Committee for Statistics.
The development of the proposed system of
automated processing of economic information
(including the accounting sub-system) is the task
of the Institute for the Automated System of
Management and Computing Techniques.

From the beginning of 1977 in all branch
ministries there came into being accounting boards
(or departments) entrusted with the task of
organising accounting and reporting in subordinate
enterprises. Until now not all enterprises have
formed an accounting service in accordance with
the approved structure: some enterprises have
created a separate accounting department, in other
enterprises it is included in the economic
administration. A substantial number of small
enterprises and budgetary institutions at the

initial stage of introducing the new accounting system had no accounting service.  For these enterprises and institutions the processing of the primary accounting documents and the compilation of the reports is undertaken by the accounting services of the branch department of the municipal and provincial government organs or by the local financial organs (which have a subdivision for questions of accounting and control).  Great difficulties, which cannot be quickly surmounted, are encountered in re-organising the system of accounting information simultaneously with the transition to the new conditions for the planning and management of the national economy.  However, at the end of 1977 nearly 95 per cent of all state enterprises and institutions undertook the accounting and presented the annual report although there were no more than half the required number of accounting workers.  For the first time there were compiled summary balance sheets and reports for all ministries and departments and for the entire country.  The data provided an important information basis for the preparation of the planned tasks and the State Budget, for the economic analysis of the indicators of the economic activities, for the realisation of control, etc. The product cost indicators obtained from the accounting and reporting data for the first half of 1978 were used for the re-examination of the current and the determination of new, state wholesale and retail prices.

As well as carrying out substantial organisational measures for the introduction of the new system of accounting into all branches of the national economy, the National Accounting System Administration of the State Committee for Finance, and also the branch accounting services, took great steps to improve the methodology and the forms of organisation, and to introduce modern means of information processing.  And, it continued to make more precise the methodological regulations concerning the composition and the economic content of the individual positions of the accounts charts in the light of the regulations on planning, financing and credit facilities.  The gradual transfer of enterprises and ministries to the principles of economic accountability (partial and full) brought about substantial changes in the composition and content of the forms and indicators of the accounting reports. To the reports have been added a supplement containing indicators revealing the manner of calculation of the payments to the State Budget, the credit relations with the National Bank, movement on the amortisation fund, profitability of the major types of products, etc. The grouping of items on the balance sheet has been clarified with the aim of providing a more realistic reflection of the enterprise's means and the sources of their formation in accordance with their economic content and designated purpose. For the experimental enterprises there were added to the report supplementary monthly indicators on plan performance for output realisation and profits and a schedule of withdrawn resources. Other aspects of accounting and reporting were revised in the light of the demands of the planning, finance, credit and other organs concerned with the development and improvement of the economic mechanism for the management of economy.

In prospect is serious work for making the basic regulations on accounting and reporting more precise in relation to the separate branches and types of economic activities (construction, agriculture, trade, transport, etc.) because the current instructions do not deal with the organisation and operation of accounting, especially in conditions of economic accountability.

At the present time the National Accounting Administration of the State Committee for Finance, together with interested ministries and departments, has prepared a chart of accounts for agricultural co-operatives and drawn up a series of regulations for accounting for the economic activities of transport enterprises, external trade, wholesaling and other types of economic activities.

One of the outstanding sections of economic work in enterprises is the planning, accounting and calculation of output cost. From the first days of the transfer to the new conditions of economic management the central and branch organs of management and a special commission gave much attention to working out methods of planning, expenditure accounting and product cost determination. In 1978 the State Committee for Finance distributed to all ministries the general recommendations for the classification of cost items and elements of production expenditure for industrial enterprises, construction, agriculture, transport and trade. There was provided an example showing the accounting for direct expenditure, the method of accounting and distribution to units of output for indirect expenditure, the valuation of work-in-progress and the summarisation of expenditure accounting. On the basis of these recommendations a number of ministries prepared branch instructions on the special features of planning, accounting, output cost determination and sent them for re-examination to the special commission. The work of expenditure accounting and output cost determination improved significantly in leading enterprises of the sugar, chemical and other leading branches of industry.

One of the most difficult problems is the provision of highly-qualified cadres to accounting services. The training of economic and managerial cadres, including accounting, were expanded considerably - advanced economic courses, seminars for raising qualifications, special schools for the rapid preparation of specialists, etc. There was increased recruitment of students for the accounting specialism in the economics faculties of universities and in intermediate specialist educational establishments. Students were sent to study in advanced educational establishments of the USSR and other socialist countries.

Taking account of the difficult cadres situation and the large number of small enterprises, economic organisations and budgetary institutions, the National Accounting System Administration, together with the local financial organs and the branch administrations (departments) of the local organs of state power, gave much attention to the question of the centralisation of accounting. There has been conducted a survey of the most rational forms of accounting organisation. The creation of centralised accounting in socialist countries has been studied. In several regions and provinces there have been attempts to organise specialised enterprises (centralised accounting) for the processing of accounting information and the provision of accounting services to local enterprises and institutions. Cuban specialists consider the most acceptable form of centralised accounting at the first stage to be the creation of inter-branch centralised accounting for a district or town.

The mechanisation and automation of accounting has proceeded in two directions:

1. On the basis of keyboard calculating machines, especially the Askot. At the time of introducing the new accounting system all the recommended documentation (primary documents, accounting registers and reporting forms) were adapted to the requirements of mechanised data processing.

2. The preparation of the necessary conditions for the creation of the accounting sub-system in the context of electronic data processing and automated systems of management. Much attention has been given to the automatic compilation of summarised indicators. Already in 1978 those ministries with electronic data processing compiled summarised reports automatically. For example, the summary balance sheet for the first half of the year for separate types of activities and branches of the economy (i.e. ministries) was compiled with the help of electronic data processing.

At the present stage the introduction of mechanised forms and methods of accounting lack a systematic character and do not embrace all sections of accounting.
One of the difficult problems is the regularisation, simplification and unification of primary accounting documents. The statistical organs have undertaken much work in studying the current documents for all types of activities in enterprises so as to carry out in the near future a radical reconstruction of the primary accounting system. The State Committee for Statistics has drawn up recommendations for a re-examination of the terms used in primary documentation and prepared an album of model standardised documents for primary accounting for the guidance of statistical organs and branch ministries.

## Towards an Appraisal

Derek Bailey

In Cuba, following the overthrow of the Batista regime in 1960, the control of industrial enterprises was entrusted to three organisations.

The National Institute of Agricultural Reform
(INRA) controlled enterprises concerned with
livestock and agricultural produce. The Ministry
of Public Works controlled the industries
connected with construction and building
activities.  The remaining industrial enterprises
were controlled by the Ministry of
Industry.  Guevara became the minister for the
latter industry.
    From 1960 the 'budgetary system of financing'
was developed within the Ministry of Industry for
application in the enterprises under its control
and the method was sanctioned officially in the
Law Regulating the Budgetary System of Financing
Government Operated Enterprises.  The enterprises
controlled by the National Institute of
Agricultural Reform and the Ministry of Public
Works implemented the concept of economic
accountability.  Consequently, two distinctive
systems of industrial organisation, and of
accounting for industrial activities, co-existed
in Cuba.  The advantages of each system became a
matter of debate between their respective
protagonists.  Within Cuba the debate was won by
Che Guevara and his supporters.
    The outcome of the debate overtook the work,
already put in hand, to establish a uniform
accounting system.  Juce-Plan (the Central
Planning Board) had established a Committee for
the Study of a Uniform Accounting System for State
Owned Enterprises.  A scheme in outline was
devised and passed over for implementation by the
Ministry of the Treasury.  In 1961 the Department
of Accounting Methods and Systems of the Ministry
of the Treasury issued guidance on the operation
of the proposed systems.  However, that system was
not introduced into the enterprises controlled by
the Ministry of Industry.
    Consequently, with the reorganisation of
industrial management during the middle of the
nineteen-seventies a fresh start in accounting
uniformity became both inevitable and necessary.
    The form of accounting applied in Cuba prior
to 1976 had been in large measure influenced by a
conception of the accounting task developed by Che
Guevara [1]  and introduced into Cuban industrial
enterprises when he was in charge of the Ministry
of Industry.  Under the system of administration
of industrial activity then developed:

    - the income and expenditure of industrial

> enterprises was incorporated into the state
> budget
>
> - the national bank acted as the 'cash
>   register' for the national economy
>
> - a simplified system of clerical account
>   record-keeping introduced: 'All our efforts
>   must be geared towards simplifying the
>   administrative task of accounting and
>   control...'.

Guevara's approach to the utilisation of accounting in a socialist economy had an affinity to the ideas expressed by Lenin [2] in his writings during 1917-18 and reflected in accounting practice in Soviet Russia in the period immediately following the October Revolution. [3]

Che Guevara gave consideration to the problems of how to measure the economic performance of enterprises following the socialist revolution. He necessarily disagreed with a commercial evaluation of enterprise performance [4] but went further in regarding the concept of economic accountability applied in the USSR to be inappropriate to Cuban conditions. He held the social function performed by an enterprise to be more relevant to the construction of a socialist society than its performance measured in the terms of monetary profit-or-loss. Consequently, the overall results of enterprise operation were not determined within an accounting framework.

But, once the social worth of the enterprise's operations had been established, attention was directed to the measurement of the cost of output, its control and reduction:

> 'What we are really interested in is the
> enterprise's success, over a long period of
> time, in lowering production costs'. [5]

He did not take an insular view upon the scope for cost comparisons. As a bench-mark, for a developing economy with a dependency upon foreign trade Guevara argued for the necessity of comparing the local costs of output with prices upon the world market:

> '... we understand of course the socialist
> world where prices have a purely mathematical
> function, serving as measuring rods'.

Diagram 1: Organisation of Accounting in the Cuban Republic

| State Committee for Finance | State Committee for Statistics | Institute for the Automated System of Management and Computation Techniques |
|---|---|---|

National Accounting System Administration

Development of system of primary accounting documentation

Design of system for automated processing of economic (including accounting) information

General Methodology of Accounting

Organisation of Accounting in Industry and Trade

Organisation of Accounting in Agriculture, Construction, Transport etc.

Organisation of Accounting in Budgetary Institutions

Mechanisation and Centralisation of Accounting

Industrial Branch Ministry

Accounting Administration

Enterprise

Accounting Service

← accounting system operations →

← accounting systems design →

He emphasised the importance of the working collective being concerned with production costs and visualised an incentive system related to cost savings (and not to profits). [6]

There are a number of reasons why accounting may be reckoned of lesser importance in the first phase of post-revolutionary economic reconstruction. Firstly, as matters of both immediate and major importance, attention is concentrated upon the strategic decisions of economic development. For making these decisions political and social, as well as economic factors are taken into consideration. Presumably, only the revolutionary leadership is in a position to determine the appropriate weights to be assigned to each of these three classes of qualitatively diverse factors. The danger, as Guevara acknowledged, was that inept investment decisions could be, and were, taken. Secondly, there were a number of circumstances that simultaneously undermined the utility of cost data for the comparative evaluation of enterprise performance and prevented it from being used to guide the actions of operational management. There were imperfections in the system of economic organisation (e.g. defects in the planning procedures resulting in planning directives being countermanded), the disruption of supplies from overseas as a result of the economic blockade, the poor internal organisation of supplies, inadequate maintenance of productive equipment and the lack of stable trading relationships among enterprises. The cumulative effect of these shortcomings was disrupted and irregular production, so resulting in abrupt changes in the level of largely uncontrollable costs. Thirdly, an insufficiency of trained personnel. There was a lack of trained administrators to organise cost record-keeping and to undertake operational cost analysis. [7] Cuban managers had little experience in the use of accounting data. [8]

At the First Congress of the Party held in January 1976 in Havana, Fidel Castro announced the New System of Economic Management in which central planning was to be combined with a measure of autonomy for enterprises. Further, an attempt was to be made to establish a coherent relationship among prices, cost, earnings and profitability. Consequently, it would become necessary to determine enterprise results and, for this purpose, a new system of accounting was needed.

Previously, there had been accounting without
accountability. That is, hitherto enterprises had
maintained a record of their transactions but
there had been no concept of accountability for
economic performance. Now economic calculus was
to be introduced.

Every enterprise in the sphere of material
production was now expected to recoup its
expenditure from income and the implication was
that unprofitable enterprises would not continue
to be subsidised.

The new system of accounting in Cuba is
modelled on the organisation and practice of
accounting in the European socialist countries.

The Cuban accounts chart differs from the
Soviet accounts plan in two respects. Firstly, it
employs the decimal system in the classification
of the accounts. Secondly, the grouping of the
accounts does not follow the cycle of production
and distribution. Instead, the accounts for the
operating incomes, expenditures and results are
grouped separately from the accounts for balance
sheet items. It is a distinction commonly
employed in the accounts charts introduced into
West European countries. The first four classes of
the Cuban accounts plan appear to be closely
similar to the first four classes of the Hungarian
accounts plan. [9] Both accounts charts comprise
nine classes of accounts but the Hungarian
accounts chart contains four classes for outlays
(whereas the Cuban accounts chart contains but one
class) and does not have a class for results. In
fact, the general structure of the current Cuban
accounts plan corresponded to that of the accounts
plan issued in 1961 by the Cuban Ministry of the
Treasury.

An American influence may be detected in the
retention of cost centres for the classification
of production expenditures. The 1961 accounting
plan provided for the cost of production to be
structured as follows:

raw and other (i.e. processed) direct
materials

indirect materials

fuel and power for production purposes

labour (direct)

labour (indirect)

social security contributions

amortisation

other production expenses (e.g. purchased services)

It may be assumed that a somewhat similar analysis of production cost is now employed. [10]

Under the proposed reorganisation of the national economy, as set out in the Resolution on Economic Management and Planning [11] adopted at the First Congress of the Party, the primary task of every socialist enterprise would be 'to cover expenditure out of income and to yield a profit'. Interest and other obligations (e.g. to the State Budget) were to be met from the profits. And, from the profits were to be financed incentive funds to cover the costs associated with the introduction of new technology, the manufacture of new products, research and development, the increased output of goods for export, and import substitution. For the evaluation of enterprise performance there were to be used the indicators of output (volume, composition, quality), productivity, cost, profit and profitability. For the realisation of these objectives a number of conditions were required to be fulfilled:

1. the establishment of a receipts and disbursements system in the state sector. It was proposed to extend commodity-money relations among the state enterprises. For organisations whose activities were financed wholly from the State Budget it was proposed that purchase-and-sale relations be established with suppliers.

2. the creation and establishment of a national accounting system.

3. the creation of a system of taxation. The services of revenue for the State Budget were to become turnover tax, planned profits, social security contributions, 'the centralised share of the sinking fund'.

4. the implementation of an adequate price system. The prices for enterprises and

wholesalers were to be based upon 'the expenditure of socially necessary labour power' but were 'to differ from value to allow for a margin of profit'. Retail prices were to be 'fixed with an eye to the social use-value of the goods and services in Cuba in relation to the nature of the needs to be satisfied' and 'to achieve a national financial equilibrium through an adequate correspondence between the population's income and expenditure'.

5. the reorganisation of the banking system (especially the use of credit as an instrument of economic management). It was proposed that in every instance the granting of credit should be preceded by a bank analysis of the financial state of the enterprise. The main purpose for the provision of bank credit would be 'to cover part of the circulating assets'. The provision of bank credit was to be based upon 'the principle of refund and the payment of interest', with the rate of interest to be 'fixed in accordance with the conditions of each development stage and the purpose for which the credit required, the branch of industry involved, etc.'.

6. the rational creation and organisation of enterprises for their gradual incorporation into the economic accounting system.

7. the setting of standards for inventories, supply, consumption, labour inputs and the regulation of circulating assets.

Thus, the development of the national system of accounting was one of a number of interrelated measures associated with the introduction of commodity-money relations among state enterprises and intended to promote improved efficiency in their operation.

The new system of accounting introduced into Cuba represents the first instance of Soviet accounting practices being adopted outside Euro-Asia. It may be assumed that Cuba's experience will be watched closely by other developing countries adopting a non-capitalist road to economic development. And, by developing countries in which, for various historical reasons, there is a considerable state

73

participation in economic development.

## NOTES AND REFERENCES

1. See, for example, Che Guevara's articles on Production Costs, Neustra Industria Economica, Ano 1, No. 1, June 1963; On the Budgeting System of Financing, Neustra Industria Economica, Ano 2, No. 5, February 1964; Socialist Planning, Neustra Industria Economica, Ano 3, No.12, April 1965.

2. See, for example, V.I. Lenin's The State and Revolution, Can the Bolsheviks Maintain State Power?, The Immediate Tasks of the Soviet Government.

3. Say, from December 1917 to March 1919. That is, from the commencement of an attempt to organise monetary accounting on a new basis suited to Soviet conditions until the proposal to introduce non-monetary accounting gained the ascendancy with the acceleration of currency inflation from March 1919.

4. It is a sine qua non of socialist thought that a merely commercial evaluation of enterprise performance is invalid when considered from a societal viewpoint.

5. Cf. China following the Cultural Revolution. 'Since "the notion of 'efficiency' or 'rationality' ... has no meaning until the underlying basis of social values is comprehended". What remained was the problem of lowering costs once this concept of efficiency had been established'. S. Andors, China's Industrial Revolution (Robertson, London, 1977), p.217.

6. Guevara considered that profits-related bonus schemes for workers would foster personal attitudes inimical to the construction of a socialist society.

7. Cuban accountants were 'among the first professionals who denied support to a communist government and have left the country in a proportion which is higher than in any other profession', C.A. Salas, Accounting Under Communism (Arthur Sandersen, Chicago, 1962), p.iii.

8. Following the revolution many skilled administrative personnel left Cuba, Guevara cited, as an example, a North American controlled nickel extraction company in which none of the departmental managers were Cuban prior to the revolution.

9.  R.L. Scholcz, <u>The Development of Accounting in Hungary since 1946</u> (Academy of Accounting Historians, Georgia, 1976).

10. Within the enterprises controlled by the Ministry of Industry, according to Guevara, during the nineteen-sixties costs were divided into raw materials, other direct materials, indirect materials, labour costs, depreciation, social security contributions.

11. <u>Granma</u>, 11 January 1976.

Chapter Five

## ACCOUNTING IN CZECHOSLOVAKIA

A.V.V. Hercok

## Introduction

The national economy in a socialist country is a
complex and centrally managed system required to
fulfil the goals set on behalf of the whole of
society. The social ownership of the means of
production creates favourable pre-conditions for
the optimal functioning of its techno-economic
basis of the socialist economy. Individual
segments of the national economy (e.g.
enterprises) are endowed with relative economic
independence, and, by using their initiative,
carry out as efficiently as possible the delegated
economic functions.
    The economic information system (EIS) records
the actual process of socialist reproduction and
is a management instrument of the whole process.
As an instrument for the management of the process
of reproduction, it is supplemented by such
instruments as planning, economic analysis,
financing, etc. However, the EIS occupies an
important position amongst all the other
instruments of economic management. It gives
information in respect of the economic process not
simply by reporting passively, but in such ways
that the information may facilitate the management
of the economy, as a whole or in part, and exert
an active influence on people's work.
    The EIS has three sub-systems, viz., (1)
technical, e.g. prices, kilograms, pieces of
machinery, hours, (2) statistical, which is
classified into typical groupings, e.g. economic,
cultural, demographic, and (3) accounting. The
present aim is to indicate the structure of the
system of accounts and the functional importance
of the discipline of accounting.

The Government is not only a political instrument but also an economic instrument. The Government, as the central instrument for the management of the economy, is linked to the economic units, where the actual economic process takes place, through a range of intermediate managerial organisations. The types and number of these intermediate organisations depend on the needs of the economic sector and the degree of economic independence allowed to an economic unit. The Government sets up various organisations, endows them with a certain degree of economic power and independence, and entrusts them with the fulfilment of specific economic objectives. Production targets, and norms for resource usage are determined by a plan. An economic unit has wide economic autonomy, and is allowed to exercise initiative, provided it remains within the framework of the plan. On one hand, the activity of an economic unit is planned and the process of realising the plan is controlled and analysed; and on the other, the economic unit's contribution to society is assessed. The two perspectives of viewing an economic unit are inseparable.

## Types of Economic Units

There are two basic types of economic units, viz.,

1. enterprises operated on the chozrazcot system;

2. budgetary, or non-profit organisations.

The latter organisations will be touched upon only briefly.

Chozrazcot enterprises may take several forms:

1. National corporations: in commerce and industry;

2. Municipal (district) enterprises: for local transport, certain retailing activities, e.g. drinks, vegetables, repairs and maintenance;

3. Co-operative enterprises: in agriculture, and retailing, (e.g. groceries, drinks) and for small manufacturers (e.g. shoes, leather goods);

77

4.  <u>Limited companies</u>: for units engaged in foreign trade.

In co-operative enterprises the means of production belongs to the collective of members. In agricultural co-operatives the land belongs to individual members, but the produce to the co-operative; the land of individual farmers has not been nationalised. For other enterprises the means of production entrusted to them as agents, the state remaining the sole owner of such means.
Enterprises may establish co-operation/ participation groupings in areas of common interest, e.g. research, market developments, purchasing. Such groupings are called <u>gesce</u> from the French <u>gestion</u>.
The totality of enterprises is divided into the economic sectors of industry, commerce (distribution), mining, agriculture, building, transport and finance.


## Broad Aspects of Management

The Government, led by the Communist Party (CP) directs and co-ordinates all economic activity through long term and five-year plans although their actual implementation relies heavily on short-term operating plans.
Enterprises are managed and controlled by industrial ministries that provide the supporting technical, research and administrative services. For example, the ministry of chemical industry manages 40 units, ranging from paper manufacture, oil refining, paints, to industrial gases, and spreading over hundreds of individual factories. The minister appoints a manager who has the sole responsibility for the efficient running of an enterprise and only in exceptional cases may be overruled by a higher authority and then only through him. Each enterprise is divded into several typical sections or departments - e.g. technical, production, economic, commercial (selling, purchasing, delivery).
There are virtually no private capitalistic enterprises in the country, unlike in Poland or Yugoslavia.
The manager of an enterprise has the sole responsibility for its management and its representation vis-a-vis third parties. He formally agrees, orally and in writing, that he

will carry out his duties in accordance with state interests. Large enterprises have one, or several deputy managers, who usually are ranged in order of responsibility. Both the manager and his deputies are entered on a register and have statutory authority both internally and externally.

Specific functional areas are managed by assistant managers who have full responsibilities for activities within their functional sphere. The manager determines the range of their authority, including dealings with third parties.

The manager is assisted by a number of advisory groups:

(a)  advisory council composed of assistant and deputy managers and a trade union representative;

(b)  techno-economic council composed of engineering, economic, administrative, academic, and research specialists and union representatives.

Nominations for membership are proposed by the manager and discussed with the enterprise section of the CP and the trade union. The membership should not exceed 15-25 members. The council may make recommendations only but, in cases of disagreement with the manager, it has the right of appeal to higher authorities.

The manager concludes a labour contract between the enterprise and the trade unions' committee. Rights and duties, including workers' participation on a consultative basis in the running of an enterprise, are included in the contract. Central bodies thrash out differences that may arise.

Material involvement by the workers in the success of the enterprise is linked with the administration of a manager's fund, financed from profits and available for a wide range of purposes, e.g. health, culture, sport, recreation, welfare. The trade unions participate in the administration of the fund on a consultative basis.

## Chozrasvennyj Razcot (Chozrazcot)

This is a household word in socialist economics, but defies exact translation. The main function of the chozrazcot system is the achievement of planned activity whereby private and social interests are fused within, and through, the operations of an enterprise. The fulfilment of a plan reflects the satisfaction of society's needs. A chozracot organisation operates in the market, has an autonomy within the boundaries and format, determined by the objectives of a socialist state and subject to the chozrazcot system.

There are four features that characterise the system, viz:

1.  The economic autonomy is realised through the allocation by the State of capital and circulating funds to enterprises for the conduct of the planned operations. The enterprises are responsible for the economical use of the resources. The revenues from sales are required to cover all the costs incurred and provide resources for expansion.

2.  Material involvement of the people in the operating process. The material involvement is regulated at the individual level by a system of bonus wages and at the enterprise level by a policy of profit retention for social purposes in a manager's fund.

3.  The law of value is used to express the notion that quantities of individual labour in goods approximate the socially-necessary quantities of labour.

    The working of the law of value, i.e. the allocation of socially-necessary labour amongst the branches of economic activity in accordance with their respective social weights points to the establishment of prices of goods in accordance with the quantities of labour allocated to their production. But cost of production cannot be either the sole or the main criterion in the formation of prices. The relative prices of goods must correspond to their relative values and not to relationships flowing from own costs. Hence, the planning of pricing policies at all levels of the economic process must express, within tolerable limits, objective value relationships in the economy.

4.  Strict control over the allocation, deployment and recoupment of funds, i.e. the so-called

money control. An enterprise's activity is
decided centrally and locked into the State
Budget. In the plan, for each branch of the
economy down to individual enterprises, there
are set (1) norms (standards) scientifically
estimated for each item of costs and (2)
selling prices for planned products.

Funds necessary for the operations of an
enterprise come from three main sources, viz.

1) Centralised
   Funds supplied from the State budget and
   controlling organisations, (i.e.
   ministries, industrial trusts). These may
   be funds for permanent or temporary use.

2) Decentralised
   Funds generated by enterprises and
   permitted for use in operations or for
   social purposes such as workers' holiday
   homes, soccer teams, etc.

3) Credit
   Funds generated by people's savings,
   temporary surpluses accumulated in
   enterprises and in State budgets. These
   funds are available for use in accordance
   with the needs of the national economy and
   of chozrazcot enterprises.

   The Banking system is centralised, the main
bank being the State Bank in which is kept for
each enterprise a current account for recording
all operating revenues and expenditures.
   Profits retention (i.e. internal financing),
profits appropriation (i.e. into the State
budget), depreciation rates and control over
amortisation funds, are issues discussed and
settled centrally in the various ministries. In
other words, each enterprise, or group of
enterprises, has a model profile and receives
funds in accordance with such a model. Individual
enterprises have limited freedom of action and
must operate within the profile and planned norms.
   Summarising, it can be said that the
chozrazcot system rests on the following
propositions:

(i)     the economic autonomy and expected
        initiative of enterprise,

(ii)    the exercise of money control and

(iii)   the material involvement of the labour
        force.


## Accounting System

'Accountancy has two aspects - recording
and economic.  One can thus describe
accountancy as (1) a system that records
economic data, and (2) an economic
function carried out by accountants who
exploit accounting information for the
analysis of economic events and the
planning of economic decisions.
Accountancy as a management function in
an enterprise  is supported by an
accurate information system.  The two
aspects are interconnected, but the
economic aspect is dominant.  Otherwise
an information system becomes ineffective
and self-indulgent.' [1]

The above quote underlines the important role
played by the accountant in a planned economy.
Apart from his technical role as an accountant, he
has become the controlling agent in all areas of
economy, budgeting, accountability and financial
discipline.  The dual responsibility, as accountant
bookkeeper and as accountant-controller, is  under-
lined by a similar duality of accountability. [2]
He is responsible to management of his enterprise
for the accountancy functions and to the
supervising authorities for the controlling
functions.  The supervising authorities are the
Ministry of Finance, relevant economic ministries
and the Bureau of Statistics.


## Development of the Discipline

The discipline of accountancy has a distinguished
tradition.  The old cameral system of accounting
was in use for centuries and Czech practitioners
made valuable contributions to its operating
techniques.  Double-entry accounting was adopted
by enterprises very early in the last century.  In

1912 appeared a text, Theory and Practice of Accountancy, [3] that was comparable with similar publications in other countries. A School of Business Studies was founded in Prague in 1920 with accountancy forming one of the specialisations.

The theory and practice of accountancy in the country reflected and contributed to current European thought. An influence was exerted by American developments in accounting practice such as standard costing and the use of cost centres and profit centres.

Schmalenbach's Kontenrahmen, a pioneering work on accounting classifications and systems, and his thoughts on the accounting discipline were studied and applied. The occupation period contributed to the wider use of the Kontenrahmen.

After 1948, with the coming of socialism and extensive nationalisation, the existing systems were found to be well suited to the provision of information on and control over economic performance.

The existing systems of accounts in individual business sectors, (i.e. industrial, wholesale, retail and overseas trade, finance, and the non-business sector, (e.g. communes, districts, non-profit organisations), were merged step by step into a system of economic information embracing all organisations at all levels of activity. The system of traditional financial accounting was integrated with managerial accounting and adapted to link with the social and economic indicators, (i.e. social or national accounting). By 1971 all organisations, both chozrazcot and budgetary, at all levels, were embraced in an integrated socio-economic and financial information system.

There is no difference between the socialist and capitalist methods of accounting from the theoretical point of view. Both use the double-entry method handed down throughout the centuries since its initial exposition by L. Pacioli.

The balance sheet shows the types and utilisation of resources and the origin of these resources. The terms assets and equities are also used.

Assets are defined as material forms of existing means of production used in co-operation with labour in the social process of reproduction. Equities represent values advanced for definite purposes from various sources that the enterprise is supposed to enlarge by reproduction.

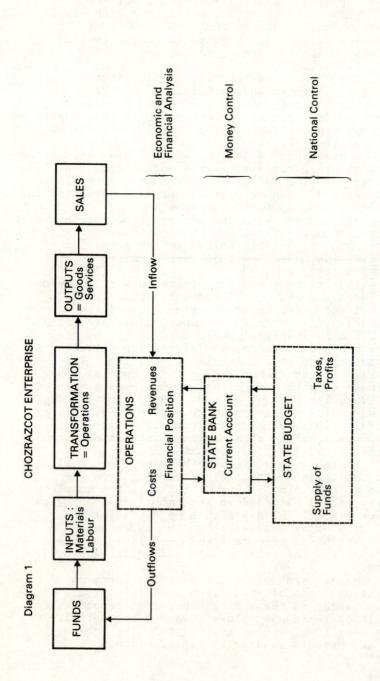

Diagram 1

CHOZRAZCOT ENTERPRISE

Diagram 2

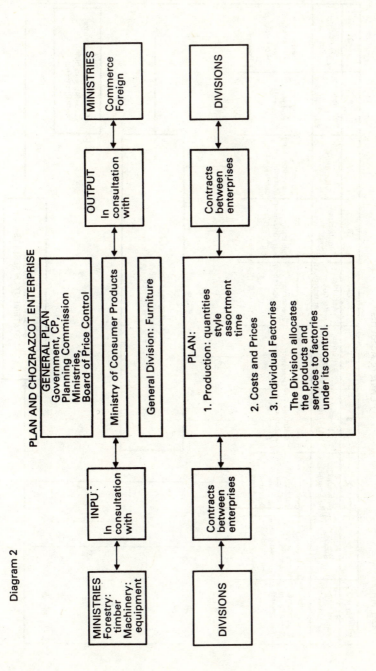

**PLAN AND CHOZRAZCOT ENTERPRISE**

**GENERAL PLAN**
Government, CP,
Planning Commission
Ministries,
Board of Price Control

**MINISTRIES**
Forestry:
timber
Machinery:
equipment

**INPUT**
In consultation
with

**Ministry of Consumer Products**

**General Division: Furniture**

**OUTPUT**
In consultation
with

**MINISTRIES**
Commerce
Foreign

**DIVISIONS**

**Contracts between enterprises**

**PLAN:**

1. Production: quantities
   style
   assortment
   time

2. Costs and Prices

3. Individual Factories

The Division allocates
the products and
services to factories
under its control.

**Contracts between enterprises**

**DIVISIONS**

Diagram 3:

Chart of Accounts

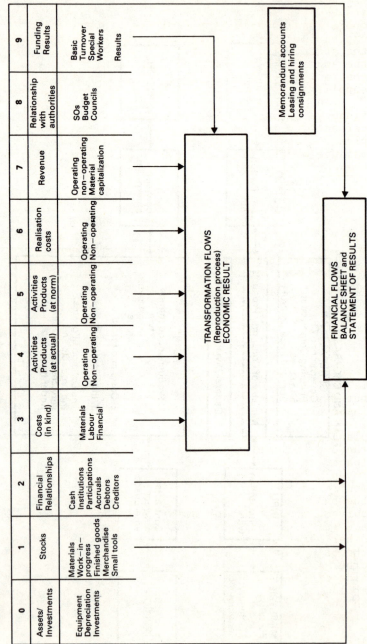

From the legal viewpoint the assets are values
at the disposal of the enterprise and used in its
operations, whereas the equities are values
expressing the responsibility of the enterprise to
the state, (i.e. to society), for the portion of
the social productive fund, and towards other
contractual parties, such as the banks and
suppliers.

The actual composition of the assets and
financial resources vested in each chozrazcot unit
reflects the requirements imposed by an economic
plan.  Diagram 4 contains a simplified example of a
balance sheet.

| Active | Passive |
|---|---|
| 1. Planned non-circulating assets | 1. Capital<br>a) Basic fund<br>b) Turnover fund |
| 2. Planned circulating assets | 2. Bank credit for planned inventories |
| 3. Liquids, debtors and other assets | 3. Temporary bank credit and other creditors (trade creditors, manager's funds and similar items) |

Diagram 4

A small portion of the depreciation allowances
is held back for necessary repairs and maintenance
but may not be used for replacements or additions.
These are determined and financed centrally.

For each enterprise there is a centrally
planned volume of production, and allocation from
the central fund of resources.  There are temporary
loans for circulating assets and especially for
inventories.  The enterprise's performance can be
monitored through the movements in various items of
the balance sheet and through the balance on the
current account at the bank.  All these movements
are reflected primarily in the circulating and
other assets, (items 2 and 3 on the active side of
the balance sheet), and through bank credits and
other liabilities, (items 2 and 3 of the passive
side of the balance sheet).  It is the practical
application of the instrument of money control as
an integral part of the overall chozrazcot system
of management and control.

Diagram 5 illustrates a typical Results
Account (i.e. profit and loss account).

### Results Account [4]

| Expenses | Plan | Actual | Revenues | Plan | Actual |
|---|---|---|---|---|---|
| Materials: | | | Entrepreneurial: | | |
|   Supplies | | |   Services | | |
|   Energy | | |   Goods | | |
|   Depreciation | | | | | |
|   Maintenance | | | | | |
|   Price | | | | | |
|     Variances | | | Changes in Stocks: | | |
| | | |   Materials | | |
| Labour: | | |   Goods | | |
|   Wages | | | | | |
|   Benefits | | | | | |
|   Travel | | | Others: | | |
|   Rents paid | | |   Sales of | | |
| | | |    materials | | |
| | | |   Interest | | |
| | | |    received | | |
| Financial: | | |   Special | | |
|   Insurance | | | | | |
|   Shortages | | | | | |
|   Fines | | | | | |
|   Fees | | | | | |
| Profit | | | Loss | | |

### Diagram 5

In accordance with the plan, profits and depreciation allowances (the rates and methods of which are determined uniformly), are either retained by the firm or transferred to the state. The greater part of the depreciation allowances go to a special Investment Bank. The bank accumulates all the depreciation funds and re-allocates them to sectors and enterprises in compliance with the overall economic plan. These can be augmented by a re-allocation of the profits originally paid into the state budget. The financial report is supported by an analysis of results prepared by superior organs. The analyses provide an explanation, in economic and financial terms of the variances between planned and actual results in terms of:

(a)   prices and costs;

(b)   volume of activity;

(c)   composition of products and services.

Factors (a) and (c) had a lesser importance until 1981 for the firms engaged in internal commerce. Because the prices for all inputs and outputs were predetermined and could not be easily varied. The composition of production, was also pre-determined for firms in the plan and could not be altered without prior consultations with the supervising organs. Consequently the factor of (b), volume of activity, attracted most of the attention when firms' performances were assessed. Firms simply tried to reach the quantities planned within the prescribed standard inputs.

Substantial changes have occurred since 1981 with the start of the seventh Five Year Plan. Individual firms will be exposed now to fluctuations in world prices. Until the end of 1980, variances arising from such changes were not reflected in the results of individual firms, but absorbed in the State Budget. However, individual firms will be now exposed to such influence and guidelines for the allocation of variances are being worked out. The situation reached in 1981, at the level of individual firms, would be thus broadly comparable to that in advanced capitalist countries with respect to financial and economic reporting.

Valuation

Original values (= historical costs) are the basis of valuation for all items in the balance sheet and for the setting of depreciation rates. Raw materials, direct labour and labour-associated overhead inputs are calculated at predetermined rates that do not change during the planning year.

All prices for products and services in the home market are predetermined in co-operation with the Board of Price Control. For this purpose, there exists detailed schedules and indices for operations and services such as labour time utilisation, rate of labour mechanisation, machine time utilisation, rate of machine utilisation. These are used for the calculation of labour intensity or productivity, and the corresponding

labour remuneration. For example, there are eight
basic classes in the engineering industry that are
being constantly revised to keep pace with
technological changes and technical progress.

Given the price schedules for basic inputs and
the allowed profit margin, the enterprises can
easily work out their own prices. The wholesale
prices are based on the costs of raw materials,
labour, overhead and a predetermined profit margin.

The retail prices add a turnover tax to the
purchase costs and predetermined retail profit
margin. The turnover tax is the major source of
state revenue. There is also a tax on wages.
There are hardly any other sources of state
revenue. Both the turnover tax and tax on wages
are collected by enterprises and transferred to the
state budget.

The accounting system records the achievement
or otherwise of such a plan and provides data that,
together with other indicators, point to causes of
variances from the plan.

## Mechanisation

Mechanical devices and computers, even if old-
fashioned, are used extensively. For example, the
whole retail trade in the country has been
computerised since 1952. A network of computer
centres run on a chozrazcot basis, handles the
classification, tabulation and summarisation
aspects of the bookkeeping process. Analysis of
summarised data is carried out by enterprises.

## Charts of Accounts

All authorities, both chozrazcot and budgetary, use
a common chart of accounts, that still shows the
traces of Schmalenbach's pioneering work.

The Ministry of Finance is the controlling and
managing authority for all aspects of accounting in
the country. Its research section develops the
chart of accounts and determines the contents of
each class and each account, the format of
financial statements and the guidelines for the
implementation of its prescriptions. There is
close co-operation between academics and research
workers in the Ministry.

## Budgetary Organisation

From the accounting viewpoint there are no
substantial differences between chozrazcot and
budgetary organisations.  The traditional cameral
accounting system was completely abolished in 1952.
A common chart of accounts, similar formats for
financial statements and common guidelines for
implementation make for a substantially unified
accounting system for all organisations.  The
budgetary organisations prepare balance sheets,
result accounts and provide for depreciation.  The
State prepares a financial balance sheet only.
Difficulties with the valuation of national
treasures have prevented the establishment of a
comprehensive balance sheet.
   Budgetary organisations in the country
represent a substantial group of organisations that
overlap with those in the chozrazcot group.  First,
there are various controlling bodies, ministries
and general management of business sectors, that
receive and disburse funds to and from both the
state budget and the chozrazcot group under their
control.
   Secondly, cities and districts have a very
large number of chozrazcot activities, called
attached economic activities that are run on
chozrazcot principles.
   The systems of accounts must distinguish
amongst the two groups with respect to:

   (a)   receipts generated by chozrazcot
         activities and those provided from the
         budget, including the provision of fixed
         assets;

   (b)   disbursements, adjusted to express
         expenses only, for both chozrazcot and
         budgetary groups;

   (c)   flows of funds, such as lending or
         borrowing, between chozrazcot and
         budgetary activities of one and the same
         authority.  It occurs when industries and
         general managements handle both budgetary
         allocations and funds for subordinate
         enterprises.

For a chozrazcot unit attached to a budgetary
organisation, there is a statement with the
following format:

Accounting in Czechoslovakia

## Summary of Economic Results

| Current loss | Current profits |
|---|---|
| Transfer of profits | Grants (all sources) |
| Appropriation for special purposes | Borrowing from parent body |
| Carried forward | Deficiency |

The country prepares summaries of social (= national) accounts for international purposes, such as those of United Nations statistics, that are based on heavily censored and adapted internal data. Such internal summaries are called Summit Balance Sheets. The financial statements of organisations, and the state financial statements are not published for public perusal.

### Concluding Observations

The discipline of accountancy plays an important role in the country's overall economic and financial information systems. Of the two functions fulfilled by accountancy the analytical (or managerial) function has increased in importance whilst the recording (or bookkeeping) function continues to decline and is being replaced progressively by mechanisation.

The conceptual framework of double-entry accounting forms the basis of the accounting system for both chozrazcot and budgetary organisations. The formats of presentation are the same as those in capitalistic countries.

Changes have occurred in terminology, although the old terms such as balance sheet, profit, amortisation etc., are slow to disappear.

Differences exist with respect to financing. There is no private ownership of productive capital, and the accounts show the financial relationship with the state (= society) and other state organisations including the financial institutions.

Central planning extends to the planning of an accounting system and the Ministry of Finance has developed a system of accounts that is common to chozrazcot and budgetary organisations.

## NOTES

1. Klozar, J. Zaklady Ucetnictvi (Fundamentals of Accountancy) SNTh, Praha, 1980, p.21.
2. Ucetni = accountant-book-keeper
Econom = accountant controller
3. Pazourek, J. Teorie a Prakse Ucetnictvi (Theory and Practice of Accountancy), Orbis, Praha, 1912.

## REFERENCES

1. Baca, J. and Tretina, F., Ucetnictvi V Prumyslovem Podniku, (Accounting for Industrial Firms), Sntl/Alfd Praha, 1981.
2. Janza, V. and Typolt, J., Otazky Tvorby Cen v Nove Soustave Rizeni Prumyslu, (Price Formation in the New System of Industrial Control, Orbis, Praha, 1958.
3. Reznicek, J., Vnitropodnikovy Chozrazcot Ceskoslovenskych Prmyslovych favodoch, (Internal Chozrazcot in Czechoslovak Enterprises), SNPL, Praha, 1956.
4. Selucky, R., Czechoslovakia, The Plan that Failed, Nelson, London, 1970.
5. Vihan, S., Uvod do Theorie Ucetni Evidence (Introduction to Theory of Accountancy), SNTL, Praha, 1953.
6. Sbornik Praci, (Compendium of Contributions), Czech Technical University, Faculty of Economical Engineering, Praha, 1955.
7. Czechoslovak Trade Unions, Review of the Central Trade Unions Council, 1971/74, pp.11-22, Praha.
8. Organisace Vyrobnich Hospodarskych Jednotek v Prumyslu, (Organisation of Production Enterprises in Industry), Orbis, Praha, 1958.
9. Problemy Nove Soustavy Planovani a Financovani Ceskoslovenskeho Prumyslu, (Problems Facing the New System of Planning and Financing of Czechoslovakian Industry), SNPL, Praha, 1957.

Chapter Six

## ACCOUNTING IN THE GDR

Gerhard Reinecke

### Background

Since its foundation in 1949, the German
Democratic Republic has embarked on a path of
socialist development requiring economic planning.
The industrial enterprises, transport system,
banks, wholesale trade and important parts of the
retail trade are nationally owned.  In agriculture
there are cooperative and state farms.
    As far as industrial output is concerned, the
country ranks among the world's leading nations.
Its economic structure is largely characterised by
the fact that there are few domestic raw materials.
Much of what is produced is exported, with the
accent on such processing industries as
engineering, the chemical industry and electronics.
    There has been an ongoing process of
industrial concentration in recent years, and while
the number of plants was about 16,000 in 1960 it
has now dropped to 5,000.  Large production units
(combines) have been established through the merger
of enterprises manufacturing major ranges of
related products.  Almost all of the country's
industrial output now comes from 157 combines which
report directly to government ministries and
another 66 combines are under the administration of
county councils.
    A standarised, comprehensive, reliable and
smoothly functioning information system at all
managerial levels is required for managing and
planning a national economy based on social
ownership of the means of production.  The current
system had two forerunners:

-   the accounting system of industrial plants which

94

emphasised the value (financial) aspect of the
reproduction process and was extremely
heterogeneous depending on the specific
conditions prevailing in the various sectors of
the economy;

- government statistics which concentrated on the
performance of the national economy and on the
material aspect of the reproduction process.

The co-existence of separate systems for
accounting and statistics often led to a
duplication in the collection of data and their
arrangement into different groupings. Consequently
the various indices and periods chosen for
comparison were not always compatible so that it
became difficult to make an integrated assessment
of economic performance. Therefore in the second
half of the nineteen sixties, the separate systems
were combined into an Accounting and Statistics
Information System which now covers all sectors of
the economy and all managerial levels and has
since proven its worth.


Structure and Function

The Accounting and Statistics Information System
is structured so as to embrace such general stages
of obtaining information as:

- data collection (primary documentation),

- systematising data according to subject areas
(and using them for detailed managerial work)
and

- data evaluation (through comprehensive analysis
and reporting).

These steps are positively linked, even though they
are separated in time and space.
The general concept is that collection and
editing must be geared to the valuation procedure.
For the operation of the system it is necessary to
catalogue the information requirements. These
information catalogues are updated to ensure that
demand is reduced to a reasonable level and data
processing programmes can be adapted in time. The
highest possible standard of clarity must be
guaranteed in formulating the information

requirements and in meeting these needs with the help of the Accounting and Statistics Information System. For this purpose the Central Board for Statistics (Staatliche Zentralverwaltung für Statistik), in collaboration with the State Planning Commission issues standard definitions, which cover certain indicators and terms. These are available as a loose-leaf collection for easy replacement and updating, and the definitions are equally applicable to planning, accounting and statistics. A major link is thus established between planning and accounting.

Primary Documentation

Primary documentation embraces the primary data, primary data carriers and primary data collection. The following concepts apply:

1. The necessary data are collected only once but evaluated for different purposes, which means that:

   i) an economic fact must be documented complete with all the characteristics needed for later evaluation;

   ii) it must be possible for the characteristics to be edited with regard to detail, scope and time to suit the requirements of evaluation; and

   iii) the amount of information needed by the bodies concerned with evaluation must have been defined and coordinated with regard to content and time.

2. Data must be systematised according to standard nomenclatures. The systematic approach adopted in a particular enterprise must be based on the nomenclatures applying throughout the national economy. Such standard nomenclatures are in use, for example, in the systematisation of products and for establishing a register of enterprises and a system of accounts.

3. The physical indicators of commodity production and the consumption factors involved must be expressed as money values according to standard procedures. This is necessary for the

aggregation of indicators at the levels both of the individual enterprise and the national economy, and also as a means for supervising economic activities with the help of the monetary unit (the mark). Standard procedures apply to the valuation of each of the various categories (e.g. machinery, supplies of material).

4. Primary documentation is subject to continuous rationalisation, and this is necessary in the interest of the national economy as a whole because:

   i)    costs must be cut while guaranteeing accurate data collection,

   ii)   data collection costs represent a major part of the total cost of information processing,

   iii)  the costs of manufacturing data carriers can be reduced by concentrating their production,

   iv)   standardised primary documentation makes it easier to use processed data more than once.

The standardization of primary data carriers goes a long way toward the implementation of the above princples. Under socialist conditions, the organisation of primary documentation is no longer a matter of company policy. Standarised documentation is desirable throughout the national economy. No objective reasons exist for having a multitude of dissimilar documents for dealing with the same economic facts, not even where different industrial processes are involved. It is with this in mind that the Central Board for Statistics has taken the lead in the project for the large-scale standardisation of primary documents. For example, standardised sets of documents are now used to account for commodities sold by industrial firms, for the labelling of goods in the retail trade and for work orders in industrial plants.

Areas

The primary data collected are assigned to any one

of three areas in the individual enterprises: (1)
The first area covers the consumption side of
production (e.g. machinery, material, labour
consumed) and the results of production (products,
material services provided). This is known as
individual accounting. It has the following major
characteristics as far as accountancy and
statistics in the various enterprises is concerned:

i) It is that stage of accounting which is
directly linked to primary documentation in
that primary documents almost exclusively are
processed.

ii) There is a particularly close link between
physical and value indicators, with the
former accounting for a much bigger share of
the entire data volume than in the case of
aggregate accounting.

iii) It has a collection and storage function for
information processing. The summarising and
aggregation of many operations of the same
kind which takes place in the area of
individual accounting, relieves integrated
accounting of collecting and editing work.
At the same time individual accounting
provides data for the analysis of specific
aspects.

iv) The fact that data of the same kind are
handled in large quantities in the process of
individual accounting makes this area
particularly suitable for the use of
electronic information processing.

v) The various fields in which individual
accounting takes place largely coincide with
areas of managerial responsibility in an
enterprise. It is therefore a practice in
many firms that the different managers who
are in charge of parts of an entire process
also supervise the related accounting and
statistics. Thus the technical manager or
senior engineer may be responsible for fixed
assets accounting while the purchasing and
sales manager could be answerable for
materials accounting. This does not detract
from the overall responsibility of the chief
book-keeper for operating a reliable and
rational system of accounting and statistics.

In all of these cases the latter must make sure that competent and proper use is made of the relevant collecting and processing methods.

The second area, integrated accounting, is concerned with the following:

i)      the costs incurred in making products and providing services, and also the complex relationship between these costs and the manufacturing process, the structure of the enterprise and the managerial process (cost accounting);

ii)     the benefit gained as a result of rationalisation and the application of scientific and technological advances (benefit accounting); and

iii)    the profit gained or loss incurred by the enterprise and balancing the use of finance against the financial sources (financial accounting).

Within the framework of accounting and statistical system of the industrial enterprise, integrated accounting can be characterised as follows:

i)      It is concerned mainly with the further processing of data which have been collected and edited in the process of individual accounting, the only exceptions being the statement of receivables and payables in the current account and the financial dealings with banks which are accounted for collectively.

ii)     It emphasises values because of the higher level of aggregation and complexity of the indicators being handled. Financial accounting is concerned with values only.

iii)    The indicators accounted for are decision-related to a great extent and are closely connected to the centralised system of statistical returns. Financial and cost accounting are normally the direct domain of the chief book-keeper.

The <u>third area</u> is known as <u>aggregate accounting</u> and does not have as systematic a structure as do individual accounting and integrated accounting.  It provides overall analyses and surveys for enterprises, with the following aims:

i)      to solve management problems,

ii)     to prepare reports from management for the workforce,

iii)    to prepare major reports for superior bodies,

iv)     to review medium-term prospects.

Aggregate accounting gives managers information which reflects the entire reproduction process of the particular enterprise.  The emphasis is on data which describe the level of development and trends prevailing in the reproduction process, and more particularly on data concerning the causes and effects of the intensification of production.  For this purpose indicators from other areas of accounting and statistics are selected, re-arranged for clarification and combined.  These figures are supplemented by verbal comments.  Most of the indicators used in aggregate accounting are obtained from financial accounting, cost accounting, benefit accounting and individual accounting.  In some cases information is derived from scientific and technical documents and other material.

Aggregate accounting provides information for managements who have to report to superior bodies and to their workforces.  In addition aggregate accounting provides information for the preparation of major managerial and planning decisions, as follows:

i)      plan fulfilment is checked and analysed;

ii)     the drawing up of economic plans is prepared and supervised;

iii)    socialist competition and its results are monitored;

iv)     the efficiency with which scientific and technological advances are used is checked;

100

v)   economic developments are compared over
     longer periods to enable long-term decisions
     to be made by management and to draw
     meaningful conclusions for the period of the
     five-year economic plans;

vi)  comparisons are made on an international
     scale.


Reporting

This is a stage which follows the systematisation
and analysis of data in the areas above mentioned.
Information concerning the economic processes which
have occurred is passed on to higher levels and also
to the workforces in various forms depending on the
recipients' needs.  It is an important link between
the individual enterprises, which are legally
independent, and the central management and
planning bodies.  There are two channels for
reporting - the centralised statistical returns
system and a system of industrial reporting  (see
Diagram 2). The former supplies most of the data
needed at higher levels of management, while the
latter exists only because the present data
processing equipment cannot provide from the
central system all the information needed by
managers.
     The industrial reporting system is used by the
various government departments to manage the
specific branches within their jurisdiction on a
scientific basis.  It is designed particularly to
meet specific requirements and to supplement the
centralised system.
     In connection with the establishment of
industrial combines independent reporting systems
have arisen within these enterprises which may be
described as in-house systems.  These cater for the
information requirements of the general manager,
his deputies and the management of the combine in
general and provide instant data.  They differ from
other systems in that:

-  they go into greater detail,
-  operate at shorter notice, and
-  contain simpler formal safeguards.

     In many cases these house systems use
preliminary data which then go to the other
reporting systems, an arrangement which to a large

extent ensures compatibility even though the scope of information and the deadlines for providing it may differ.

## Management

The body in charge of accounting and statistics at the national level is the Central Board for Statistics (Staatliche Zentralverwaltung für Statistik or SZS) which in turn reports to the Council of Ministers. It is responsible for implementing the tasks which flow from decisions adopted by the SED (the leading party of the GDR), from the Constitution and from the legal and other regulations applicable to accounting and statistics. The Board must see to it that the relevant information is collected, edited and processed in a uniform manner for all levels of management. For this purpose it enforces the regulations identifying the content, methods and organisation of accounting and statistics and ensures their observance by enterprises. The Board works closely together with the State Planning Commission, the Ministry of Finance and other government agencies, economic bodies and organisations. It has branches operating at the level of the administrative district and county, so that central and local party and government bodies can be supplied with topical and reliable information regarding the fulfilment of economic plans.

The combine which operates the computers handling many of the jobs for the Central Board for Statistics is Kombinat Datenverarbeitung.

In the enterprises throughout the economy the chief book-keeper is responsible for accounting and statistics. It is his duty, among other things, to ensure that the relevant figures and data are properly collected and edited.

## Training

Accounting and statistics is taught as a subject at all GDR universities and colleges where economists are trained. Personnel for the Accounting and Statistics Information System are trained at the Hochschule für Okonomie in Berlin, and the graduates work at the level of centralised economic management. Training for work at the level of the

combine and enterprise is provided by Karl Marx
University at Leipzig.  Most of those enrolling for
these studies will have completed training in the
areas of business administration or data processing
and spent a year of practical work in industry.
        Training at the college level is possible at
establishments located in Plauen and Rodewisch, and
most of these students have also been trained in
business administration and worked in industry.
        Apart from full-time studies, the
above-mentioned universities, institutes of
technology and colleges also offer correspondence
courses and postgraduate studies in various forms.
The Central Board for Statistics also runs advanced
training courses, particularly for chief
book-keepers.
        The job of chief bookkeeper is a suitable
model to be used in training personnel for
accounting and statistics, and students can easily
relate to this image.  For university and college
teachers it serves to illustrate the dialectics of
socialist economic management and particularly the
agreement which is sought between the interests of
the enterprise concerned, and society as a whole.
It is the main task of the chief bookkeeper to make
sure that this harmony is not disturbed in the
day-to-day operations of combines and enterprises.
For this purpose he is obliged to give the
necessary assistance to the general manager, works
manager and all other managerial levels.  There are
three areas in particular to which chief
bookkeepers must attend:

-   they must ensure that proper and full use is
    made of the nationally owned property and
    facilities at the disposal of these production
    units;

-   they should help improve efficiency; and

-   they must provide reliable data on the
    reproduction process within the framework of the
    Accounting and Statistics Information System.

        Apart from other aspects, it is these three
areas which are at the centre of university and
college training.  The aim is not to carry
specialisation too far but to teach basic concepts
so that the graduates, particularly from
universities and institutes of technology, can be
flexible in their assignments.

Mention should also be made of the high proportion of female students training for these subjects, a factor for which allowance must be made, especially during the first few years after graduation.

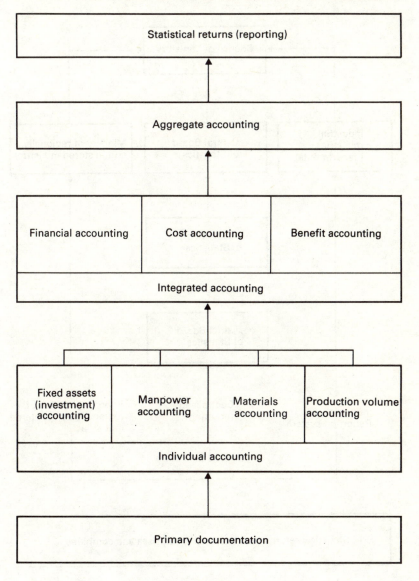

Diagram 1:

The structure of accounting and statistics in enterprises (in the industrial sector)

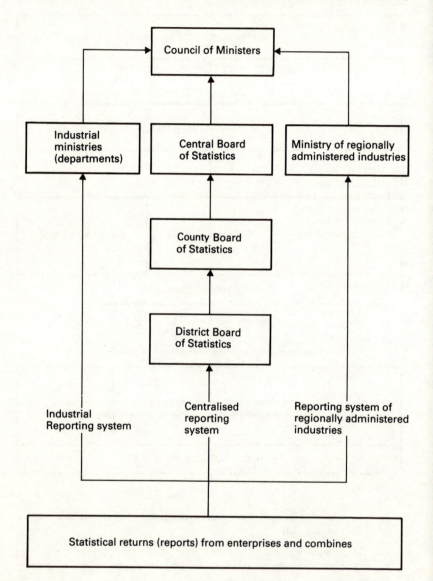

Diagram 2:

The structure and flow of information from enterprises (in the industrial sector)

Chapter Seven

## ACCOUNTING IN HUNGARY

R.L. Scholcz

In Hungary the severe post-war inflation
disorganised the practice of accounting.  The
reform and stabilisation of the value of money was
achieved through the introduction of the forint on
1 August, 1946.

> '... the accounting data expressed in the
> former pango currency could neither be
> converted into, nor compared with data
> expressed in forint ...' [1]

> 'Proper accounting activities could begin only
> on January 1, 1947.  In the development of
> accounting, from that date up to now, three
> periods can be distinguished': [2]

1946-1950 'Reconstruction of accounting, as
far as possible, in an economy
entirely disorganised through war
and inflation.  In this period were
developed the basic forms of
enterprise accountancy.' [3]

1950-1967 establishment of 'the foundations of
national economic accounting'. [4]

1968-    Introduction of 'the new system of
economic control and management ...
In this period was created the
country-wide uniform system of
accounting.' [5]

The Extraordinary Law, adopted by the
Presidium of the National Assembly, defined the
concept of accounting so as to embrace:

- double entry accounting (synthetical accounting and the related analytical registers)

- production expenditure accounting and output cost determination

- compilation of balance sheet and profits and losses report

- all types of internally used information derived from the aforementioned records.

The methodological direction of accounting is entrusted to the Ministry of Finance under which has been created the accounting methodological council, as a consultative organ, comprising 25 members nominated by the Ministry of Finance and of which:

15 proposed by the heads of ministries and state departments

10 scientific and practical workers.

The Ministry of Finance is responsible for:

- determination of the structure and content of the unified national economic accounting and, on its basis, the unified principles of the accounts plans for branches of industry

- determination of the manner of production expenditure accounting and output cost determination and for the compilation of the reported output cost computation

- devising the rules for the compilation of primary documents; verification of inventories and valuation of assets; compilation of entries in respect of inventory verification, balance sheets and profits and losses reports.

The Ministry of Finance publishes decrees on:

- conduct of accounting in enterprises and economic organisations

- verification of inventories and compilation of balance sheets in state and co-operative enterprises and organisations

- compilation of balance sheets and verification of inventories in budget financed institutions

- primary documents for enterprises and economic organisations.

In collaboration with the interested organs the Ministry of Finance establishes the procedures for:

- exaction of taxes

- formation and utilisation of material stimulation funds.

The Ministry of Finance establishes the rules for the conduct of financial audit. The financial audit embraces:

- control for the implementation of the obligations of enterprises and economic organisations to the State Budget

- control for the utilisation of resources received from the State Budget

- control for the formation and utilisation of various funds

- control for the compilation of balance sheets and profits and losses reports

- verification of the correctness of the reflection of:

  economic operations and financial results

  financial position and property status

- verification of the state of accounting and the compilation of primary documents

- control for adherence to documentary discipline.

Within an enterprise accounting is under the direction of either a deputy director (usually the economics director or the chief bookkeeper). The balance sheet is ratified by the director of an enterprise or, for co-operatives, by the general meeting of members.

Accounts plans were approved in 1947, 1951, 1955 and 1968. The distinction between balance

sheet accounts and income statement accounts was
emphasised by their being assigned to separate
classes in the initial accounts plan, abandoned in
the successor accounts plan and subsequently
reintroduced.  The second accounts plan provided
for the 'integration of financial accounting and
manufacturing accounting'. [6]  By the third
accounts plan enterprises 'were given free scope to
classify and group the costs of production with
regard to their special needs'. [7]
   The current accounts plan is comprised of the
following classes:

| Class | Purpose |
|---|---|
| 1. Basic means | |
| 2. Inventories | |
| 3. Current accounts | Compilation of balance sheet |
| 4. Funds | |
| 5. Elements of expenditure | |
| 6. Burden expense | Reflection of production expenditure |
| 7. Costs of activities | |
| 8. Cost of realised output and miscellaneous expenses | |
| 9. Realisation receipts and miscellaneous income | Compilation of profits and losses report |

   In the early years the net income of an
enterprise was determined in accordance with the
brutto principle.  That is, 'profits or losses were
... determined by deducting the expenses incurred
in the period ... from sales revenue earned in the
period...' [8]  Subsequently, from 1951, the net
income was determined in the accounting records in
accordance with the netto princple.  That is, an
adjustment was made for 'the amount of the
differences between the beginning and the ending
inventories of finished goods'. [9]

As already mentioned, in 1951 financial accounting and manufacturing, or cost, accounting were integrated into the revised accounts plan so that expenditure accounting is conducted by:

<u>Current accounts plan</u>

1. Expenditure elements     in class 5

2. Places of origin and
   types of output          in classes 6 and 7

That is, there is an accounting for both inputs (traditionally the sphere of financial accounting) and for the conversion of those inputs into outputs (traditionally the sphere of manufacturing or cost accounting).

The accounting for expenditure elements (i.e. for inputs) was adopted in the original accounts plan, being 'introduced above all for the needs of national economic planning and analysis. This information is necessary for the calculation of the national income and the construction of the inter-branch balance. The designation of the accounts of this class corresponds with these requirements.' [10]

However as Schoenfeld has observed:

'Often requirements for financial accounting and cost accounting differ considerably with respect to timing, speed, and accuracy. As a result of these incompatible demands, the idea of separating both systems has gained acceptance in Europe, particularly in Germany' during the nineteen-thirties. In the FGR capitalist enterprises use either 'the so-called unified one-cycle system (<u>Einkreis-System</u>)' or 'the so-called two-cycle system (<u>Zweikreis-System</u>) in which financial and cost accounting work routines can be separated. To operate a full-fledged two-cycle system, a connection between the two accounting cycles must be established which permits the tracing of all values.

The transfer account two-cycle system separates cost from financial data by establishing ... a complete duplication of cost accounts ... While the one-cycle system is based on a continuous flow of accounting data ... the financial accounting part of the

111

two-cycle system omits all cost accounting steps ... The duplication of all necessary accounts ... can be accomplished by either repeating those accounts directly or showing them as mirror images of the original entries. In both cases entirely separate accounting cycles are generated. The second cycle eventually yields the data as found in a one-cycle system and permits independent scheduling of accounting work based on specific departmental timing considerations.' [11]

Since 1951 the two-cycle system has been applied in Hungary. Within the structural framework of the authorised accounting system applied in all enterprises there is maintained a separation between the financial accounting and cost accounting procedures. One of either of two variants of the two-cycle sysetem are employed:

1. The costs are debited to the accounts of classes 6 and 7 with the corresponding credit entries recorded in the accounts of classes 1, 2 and 3. At the end of the quarter the expenditure elements are debited into accounts 51 and 56 and credited to account 59 Contra a/c for Expenditure Elements.

2. The expenditure elements are debited to the accounts of class 5 with the corresponding credit entries to the accounts of classes 1, 2 and 3. The costs are debited to the accounts of classes 6 and 7 and credited to account 59 Expenditure Elements Transferred.

   'With both variants of the two-cycle system the total sum of the costs debited to the accounts of classes 6 and 7 is required to be equal to the total sum of the expenditure elements.' [12]

The equality is ensured through the use of:

account 57 Deferred Composite Expenditures

account 58 Reimbursed Composite Expenditures.

A composite expenditure is one composed of more than one expenditure element. Deferred composite expenditures comprise expenditures incurred in the

Diagram 1: Scheme of interconnections of classes of Plan Accounts

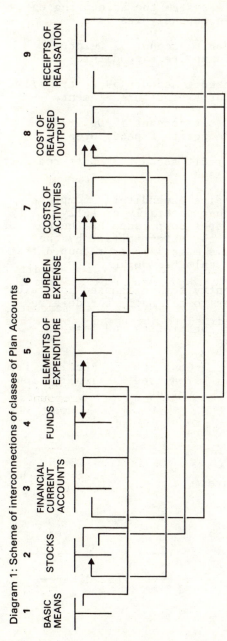

| 1 | 2 | 3 | 4 | 5 | 6 | 7 | 8 | 9 |
|---|---|---|---|---|---|---|---|---|
| BASIC MEANS | STOCKS | FINANCIAL CURRENT ACCOUNTS | FUNDS | ELEMENTS OF EXPENDITURE | BURDEN EXPENSE | COSTS OF ACTIVITIES | COST OF REALISED OUTPUT | RECEIPTS OF REALISATION |

KEY

1. Accounting for expenditure of reporting period (by elements of expenditure)
2. Accounting for burden expenses
3. Transfer of shops expenses to production accounts
4. Accounting for direct expenses
5. Transfer of undistributed expenses to accounts for financial results
6. Accounting for stocks of own production (at segment cost)
7. Transfer of value of realised articles (commodities) at segment cost (acquisition price) to results accounts
8. Accounting for receipts from realised articles (commodities)
9. Connection between results accounts

Adapted from R. Scholcz, Bukhgalterskii uchet v Vengerskoi Narodnoi Respublicke (M. 1974) p. 28

current reporting period in respect of future
periods.
     For the two-cycle system the accounting entry
for deferred composite expenditures is:

i)  for variant  I    debit account 57 Deferred
                      Composite Expenditures

                      credit account 59 Contra a/c
                      for Expenditure Elements

ii) for variant II    debit account 57 Deferred
                      Composite Expenditures

                      credit account 39 Deferred Cost
                      Items

     Reimbursed composite expenditures comprise
     expenditures either partially or fully
     excluded from output cost, such as the cost of
     spoilt output to the extent offset by the
     value of re-usable materials or recouped from
     the wages of the culpable worker.

     The accounting entry for reimbursed composite
expenditure is similar to the entry for deferred
composite expenditure.
     The structure of the profits and losses
report is as follows:

|                              | Cost of realised output | Receipts from realisation |
| ---------------------------- | ----------------------- | ------------------------- |
| Realisation of commodity output |                     |                           |
| Other realisation            |                         |                           |
| Unallocated expenditures     |                         |                           |
| Miscellaneous expenses       |                         |                           |
| Miscellaneous income         |                         |                           |
|                              | ———                     | ———                       |
|                              | ———                     | ———                       |

In outline, the structure of the balance sheet is as follows:

### Balance Sheet

| Active<br>Means | Passive<br>Sources |
|---|---|
| Written down value of basic means and capital investment (A/c 11-16 & 19 less A/c 17) | Fund for basic means (A/c 41) |
| Stocks (A/cs 21-28) | Fund for circulating means (A/c 42) |
| Financial means (A/cs 31-38) | Other funds (A/cs 43-46 and 48) |
| Basic means and stocks for cultural and communal purposes (A/cs 18, 29) | Financial sources (from A/cs 31-38) |
| | Fund of basic means and stocks for cultural and communal purposes (A/cs 418 and 428) |
| Carried forward assets (deferred expenses) (from A/c 39) | Carried forward liabilities (outstanding payments) (from A/c 39) |

In January 1966 the Ministry of Finance issued a new regulation simplifying the procedure for cost determination.  Each enterprise was given the right to select the method of output cost determination considered most appropriate for its circumstances  and also the basis for the distribution of indirect costs.

From this time the unplanned expenses were excluded from output cost and written off against the financial result of the enterprise.  Unplanned expenses comprise such items as:

- idle time losses

- monetary fines and penalties

- difference between penalties and damages received and paid for breach of contracted delivery conditions

- payment for idle time

- difference between excesses and deficiencies of over-norm stocks.

The decree reduced the range of expenses to be incorporated into output cost. There was required to be compiled both projected and post, or reported, output cost computations.

For the short-term (i.e. quarterly) cost computation it now was permitted to attribute only direct costs to individual products without the apportionment of indirect costs during the course of the year.

There was introduced the new indicator of segment cost comprising direct costs and shops expenses.

The concept of cost determination embraces both the expected, or projected, and the actual, or reported, cost computations for products, work and services.

Output cost determination is formed from the production expenditures and provides the basis for the compilation of the price calculation.

Summarising, the tasks of output cost determination comprise:

- compilation of the projected planned cost computation

- carrying out operational monitoring, and calculation, of the actual output cost and providing the information necessary for the formation of prices

- substantiation of the valuation of stocks of own production by means of an authentic cost computation

- providing to the executives of the enterprise in the current manner the necessary data on production expenditures and output cost.

By the Extraordinary Law adopted by the National Assembly since 1968 the economic organisations have been required to give attention to the creation of such manner of accounting for current expenditures so as to enable:

- formation of production expenditures

- determination of the cost of output, work and services

- preparation of calculations at the national economic level.

There is required to be undertaken once annually the determination of the actual cost of output. It is used for the study of the relationship between cost and wholesale price and the analysis of profitability.

In the majority of enterprises a substantial part of the expenses are attributed to products by apportionment, thereby reducing the precision of the disclosed cost.

The manner of cost determination is decided by each enterprise. The general instructions on the organisation of output cost determination, appended to the instructions for the application of the branch plans of accounts, are confined to general requirements, setting out the content of the various categories of cost and individual cost items.

The enterprises have freedom to select the most suitable method of output cost determination by taking into consideration:

- type of production

- organisational structure

- level of technical equipment

- character of the production process

- procedure for the documentation of economic operations.

The former requirement for the calculation of the cost of all types of output was abolished by the Ministry of Finance as too labour-consuming. It is compiled now for the finished output held in store at the end of the year.

The enterprise may compile reported cost computations monthly, quarterly, or at the end of a serial production run, for:

- determination of actual cost

- valuation of stocks of own production.

In the course of the year there may be attributed only direct costs to separate products, the indirect costs being apportioned between finished output and work-in-progress only for the compilation of the quarterly balance sheet.

The enterprise has the right to select the method for the distribution of indirect costs.

The enterprise is required to undertake such manner of cost determination as will ensure reliable information on the formation of production expenditures and the level of cost.

The Regulation on the Conduct of Accounting, ratified by the Ministry of Finance on 30 December, 1970, stated that enterprises are required to prepare, with respect to their individual plans of accounts, their own regulation on output cost determination. The regulation is required to specify:

- objects of cost determination (i.e. the cost units)

- scheme of cost determination with explanation of the content of individual cost items

- classification of shops for accounting for shops expenses and the bases for the distribution of these expenses

- description of the method of expenditure accounting and output cost determination

- periodicity for the compilation of the reported cost computation

- procedure for the compilation, verification and organisation of the flow of primary documents for the reported cost computation

- manner for verification of the correspondence of the data of the reported cost computation with the data shown in the synthetical accounts

- responsibility for the presentation and verification of the data required to be reflected in the reported cost computation.

The specimen cost structure for industrial enterprises embraces:

- total direct expenses

- segment cost

- production cost

- total cost.

The principle of economic accountability requires all expenditures to be recouped from the receipts of realisation.

Total cost embraces all the production expenditures arising in the reporting period with the exception of the expenditures recorded in A/c 89 Miscellaneous Expenses. The so-called unplanned expenses are considered to be unjustified and are excluded from output cost and written off against profits. These expenses may not be taken into consideration for the purposes of price formation.

Production cost embraces only those expenses dependent upon the enterprise. Excluded are amounts paid for the use of funds and for the reimbursement of expenditures on technical development and on repair work carried out during the repair period.

The truncated cost comprises the direct production expenditures and the shops expenses. It provides, as a measure of cost, the most close approximation to an accurate indicator of the expenditures incurred on the manufacture of individual types of products.

The preponderant part of works general expenses are fixed expenses for which only with difficulty may be found, if at all, an apropriate basis for their proper attribution to individual types of output. The expenses for the central management of enterprises are considered to be proportional to calendar time and are not distributed among individual types of output.

For demonstrating the link between shops expenses and the manufacture of individual types of products it is desirable to use a physical measure as the basis for their distribution. To improve the accuracy of cost determination the shops expenses should be divided into homogeneous groups,

119

an appropriate basis being chosen for the distribution of each group. For example, such groups might be:

- maintenance and utilisation of equipment expenses

- other shops expenses.

The bases chosen for distribution of shops expenses must accord with the instructions for price determination.

The new cost category of segment cost was introduced on 1 January, 1968. It is considered to be a valuating indicator. Thus the stocks of own production are valued at segment cost and the remaining expenses, irrespective of the volume of realisation, are written off against the financial result for the period.

Segment cost, rather than full cost, is considered to give the most useful information on the formation of cost to the executives of the enterprise.

The expenses incorporated into total output cost may be subdivided as follows:

- expenses dependent on the volume and composition of output. These expenses change in proportion to changes in the volume of output. As a rule, their amount may be established and attributed directly to the cost of the product. The direct expense component may be considered to be a completely precise part of cost and provides the basis for techno-economic decisions.

- expenses that to a certain extent are dependent on the volume and composition of output. To this group belongs, in particular, shops expenses. As a rule, these expenses may be included in the cost of individual types of output only by conventional means (by the procedure of distribution). The accuracy of the calculated cost depends upon finding the proper basis for their distribution. Product cost comprising direct costs and a portion of shops cannot be considered to be completely accurate information.

- fixed expenses, the amount of which is not dependent upon the volume and composition of output. It is difficult to find a justified basis for their distribution. If these expenses are distributed to individual types of output it

Accounting in Hungary

is impossible to consider the resulting total
cost as valid information upon which to base
economic decisions.  To this group belongs works
general expenses and non-recurring expenses.

Expenditures excluded from segment cost are
distributed among individual types of output only
at the end of the year for the compilation of the
reported cost computation, thereby reducing
significantly the labour intensity of output cost
determination.  The reported segment cost
computation is compiled at the end of the year only
for the completed output not realised (and held in
store) at the end of the reporting year.
One of the most important consequences of the
application of the indicator of segment cost is
the increase in the volume, and expansion of the
range, of products.  The enterprise is motivated to
increase the amount of realisation.  It is
encouraged to do so by the valuatin of stocks at
segment   cost because the formation of profit is
now closely connected with the realisation of
output.  It becomes necessary for the enterprise to
study closely consumer demand and the conditions in
the market and to adapt to it the assortment of
output.


REFERENCES

1.  R.L. Scholcz, The Development of
Accountancy in Hungary Since 1946, Academy of
Accounting Historians, Working Paper No.28, Georgia
State University, Atlanta, December 1976, p.1.
2.  R.L. Scholcz, loc cit.
3.  R.L. Scholcz, loc cit.
4.  R.L. Scholcz, loc cit.
5.  R.L. Scholcz, loc cit.
6.  R.L. Scholcz, loc cit.
7.  R.L. Scholcz, loc cit.
8.  R.L. Scholcz, loc cit.
9.  R.L. Scholcz, loc cit.
10.  R.L. Scholcz, Bukhgalterskii uchet v
Vengerskii Naradnoi Respublike, (M.1974), p.20.
11.  H.M. Schoenfeld, Cost Terminology and
Cost Theory:  A Study of its Development and
Present State in Central Europe, (Centre for
International Education and Research in
Accounting, Illinois, 1974), pp.29-31.
12.  R.L. Scholcz, op cit., p.20.

Chapter Eight

## ACCOUNTING IN POLAND

Alicja Jaruga

## Introduction

The socio-economic system in Poland is based on
socialisation of the means of production, trade,
communication, banks, and large scale agriculture.
[1] The country's development has thus been based
on a planned economy. The fact that a major part
of the economy has been socialised and that this
sector generates approximately 80 per cent of the
total national income has created the need to plan
and control centrally the allocation and use of
nationalised resources to meet the rising needs of
the entire society.

Central planning of the Polish economy ensures
the concentration of resources on the realisation
of the most important tasks. It makes possible a
rational division of the national income into two
parts for consumption and for investment. At the
same time the centrally planned socio-economic
system promotes a rational and fair distribution of
national income to all groups of the population.
However, detailed intervention of the central
authorities into activities of individual
enterprises is not implied. The essence of central
planning lies in mapping out the basic guidelines
for development and devising the steering
mechanisms by which the economy functions. [2]

At the first stage of economic development
there was a high degree of centralisation. The
subjection of management and control to centralised
direction was the hallmark of the socialist
economy. At that time accounting's role was
limited and attention was directed to physical
units. The market mechanism was almost totally
ignored. [3]

122

At the present stage of socialist economic
development, there is a transition from extensive
to intensive forms of development. Centrally
determined preferences are used by general planning
systems in strategic decisions of resource
allocation. However, some economic levers and
other indirect tools are also employed at the
basis of the multi-level information and control
system so as to make the economy more flexible in
terms of changing environmental conditions. [4]

## Multi-level Information and Control Systems

In the organisational structure of the Polish
economy the central authority is represented by the
Planning Commission of the Council of Ministers.
The next lower level is constituted of various
ministries. Below the ministries there are unions
of enterprises with a given branch of industry.
These are known as Large Business Organisations
(LBOs). There is a hierarchy of goals in the
centrally planned economy. [5] There are used
tasks, directives, control standards and economic
levers in order to enable the enterprises and LBOs
to optimise the overall goals of society and
harmonise the efforts of individuals and groups of
individuals.
     Information flow in multi-level management
systems of the planned economy is shown in Diagram
1. The enterprise represents the lowest level of
decision-making (i.e. Level 1).
     The state owned enterprises are allocated
means of production, granted bank loans and are
legally incorporated. The economic discretion of
state owned enterprises is the fundamental rule
for the operation of the self-financing principle
and economic accountability.
     Generally, in accordance with productive
capacity, operational tasks are recommended to the
enterprise by higher levels of management (see line
I in Diagram 1). Some of these tasks are listed
below:

- minimum quota for sale of goods and services in
  domestic and foreign markets,

- range of differentials and rate of growth for
  wages and salaries,

- taxable sales income in excess of planned volume,

- maximum expenditure on capital projects,

- maximum quotas for imports (expressed in foreign currency),

- intrabranch co-operative exchange of goods and services (minimum volume).

The enterprise, has, however, some degree of freedom in decision-making, e.g. in the new products promotion, modernising of technology.
At the present stage of socialist economic development, LBOs and enterprises are required to observe a whole set of control standards and parameters (see line II in Diagram 1).


## Control Standards

(a)   The socialised equity is given to an enterprise and should be used with at least minimum efficiency. The enterprise is obliged to pay a given percentage rate on net book value of fixed assets to the government. It should be noticed that an enterprise is obliged to make specified payments to the government for utilisation of its resources.

(b)   Rates of linear depreciation on fixed assets are established centrally.

(c)   Definite percentage rate of interest on loans for capital projects is established by government. Loans should be repaid first of all from accumulated depreciation and residual income.

(d)   Percentage rate of interest on loans for inventories is established by government.

(e)   The enterprise is obliged to contribute to the centralised social consumption fund. The contribution is calculated at a specified percentage of wages and salaries paid and charged against the enterprise's surplus.

(f)   Charges against residual income for premium fund for top management staff are regulated as

124

also the percentage <u>rate of charges against</u> <u>residual income for the enterprise's</u> <u>development fund</u>.

In addition, the relevant Ministry determines the long-term rate of charges governing contributions to the <u>costs of technical and</u> <u>economic progress fund</u>.

The main performance measures and economic levers are as follows:

(a)  <u>Value added</u> and <u>residual income</u> are considered to be the main efficiency measures of every enterprise's activities.

(b)  The level and rate of growth of the wages and salaries is related to the level and rate of growth of value added.  The relation is regulated by a special <u>reduction parameter</u> by the Ministry and given to lower levels of management while at the same time some adjustments at lower levels are allowed.

(c)  Specific <u>percentage rates</u> and methods for the calculation of income and turnover taxes are established for every enterprise and form a part of the procedure for surplus distribution.

(d)  <u>Prices, tariffs, hard currency exchange</u> <u>rates, customs duties</u> are fixed by government agencies and usually are stable over 2 - 5 year periods.

Control standards and economic levers are used to influence enterprises indirectly to increase their business efficiency.  When optimising their plans the enterprises are striving for continuous growth of value added and residual income. [6]

## Diagram 1

## Multi-Level Management

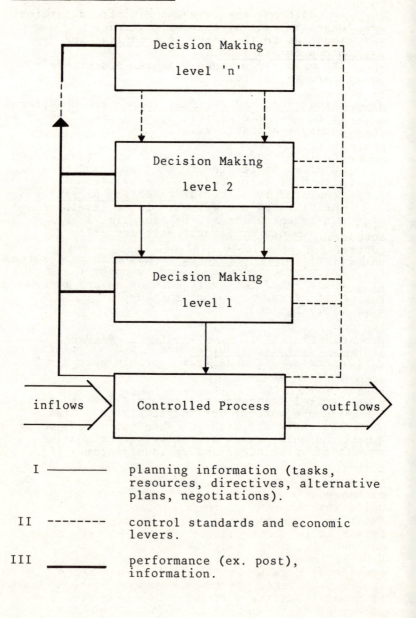

I ———— planning information (tasks, resources, directives, alternative plans, negotiations).

II - - - - - - control standards and economic levers.

III ▬▬▬▬ performance (ex. post), information.

Accounting in Poland

At the first stage of socialist economic
development, accounting was mainly orientated to
control of task performance, and acted as a
monitoring tool through the provision of feedback.
The rate of cost reduction was the measure of
efficiency. At the present time, given the
relative autonomy of LBOs and the developed
system of worker participation, accounting is
more and more orientated to the generation of
surplus. Accounting should furnish ratios
facilitating the analysis of the creation and
distribution of surplus in the context of a more
comprehensive accountability for socialised
resources. The role of accounting for decision
making purposes at LBO level is growing
continuously.

In the centrally planned economy there can be
distinguished two groups of users of the accounting
information generated in enterprises.

Planning and control for the whole national
economy (see path I in Diagram I) has different
accounting information needs from planning and
control for relatively discrete, semi-autonomous
units of business management. In response to the
first requirement, a standardised accounting and
financial reporting system has been established
for the calculation and distribution of gross
national product, value added, national income,
the compilation of input-output tables and the
preparation of a national economic balance
statement. From the point of view of the
socialised form of ownership only macro-
accounting expresses fully the effectiveness of
business operations and activities (see path II in
Diagram I).

Self-financing concept and the Balance Sheet

Both in socialist and non-socialist economies, there
are similar economic transactions based on the
exchange of commodities and money. The economic
units function as autonomous or semi-autonomous
entities. The degree of economic discretion
permitted to these entities in the Polish economy
may be lower than in capitalist countries.
However, their economic accountability has grown
considerably since the late nineteen-fifties. In
the Polish system the state-owned enterprises act
as separate entities in spite of the state
ownership of the nationalised means of production.

The economic discretion of state-owned enterprises is a fundamental rule of economic accountability. It is an expression of the self-financing principle. For this reason there are used such economic levels as cost, income, price, credit, interest and many other nominal measures. Although formally similar, these economic levers are generally different in content in capitalist countries as compared with socialist countries.

State-owned enterprises are allotted fixed assets (a part of entire social resources) and their equivalent is reflected by the state fund for fixed assets. To ensure at least a minimum level of ifficiency, the enterprise is obliged to make periodical payments at a given percentage rate to the central government budget.

Current assets continuously attached to operations (approximately 50 per cent of inventories), as distinguished from social resources, are equivalent to the state fund in current assets. To finance the remaining part of the total current assets the enterprise should apply for loans from the National Bank. However, outstanding suppliers' payables may decrease the credit needs of the enterprise.

In addition to the current business operations every state enterprise should conduct a variety of activities for the benefit of its employees and their dependants. Special purpose funds for employees are created through charges into cost, e.g. for housing fund, social welfare fund and incentives fund.

The enterprise may designate a part of its residual income for an expansion of its fixed and current assets through the creation of a development fund. The development fund may be further increased by depreciation on fixed assets if their purchase has been financed from its own (surplus) resources. For more extensive development needs, the enterprise is allowed to take long-term banks loans, repayment of which should be made from depreciation and from development fund.

For major centralised capital projects, usually of great national economic significance, depreciation should be transferred to centralised funds of the government.

Enterprises are obliged to follow standard financial rules. The balance sheet structure is intended to reflect and assist the verification of observance of the standard rules of the financial system and to disclose the financial position.

Particular assets groups correspond with appropriate sources for their financing.

## Valuation Rules

In Poland valuation principles are uniform. The relatively rare changes made in prices can result only from decisions of the government authorities.

Immovable and movable assets are valued at their acquisition costs (i.e. at historical cost). General revaluations of the book value of fixed assets are based on a centrally determined uniform index of prices to assure objectivity in physical replacement of fixed assets. The change of historical value affects only the book value of fixed assets and the state fund for fixed assets.

Assets which do not include labour, (e.g. land, mineral resources) are not considered as commodities and are not subject to valuation (excluding private farming).

Depreciation is computed generally on a straight line basis. Depreciation rates are uniform for particular classes of fixed assets but the appropriate authorities may change the depreciation rates when necessary. Charging depreciation into costs starts, as a rule, in the first month after acquisition of fixed assets and ends when the accumulated depreciation is equal to the gross book value of the fixed assets.

Inventories of materials are valued at cost of purchase. Changes in inventory valuation caused by new prices do not influence the financial results. The changes occur only at the turn of the year. General changes in prices are considered to be an exogenous factor when adjusting and evaluating the financial results of an enterprise and are offset by an adjustment to the state fund (for current assets). New prices are fixed by central authorities and are relatively stable.

Finished goods inventories are valued at full historic cost basis. When actual cost exceeds the net realisable value budget cost is used for valuation. Work in process inventories are valued at full cost.

Labour is not considered to be a commodity in Poland. To ensure the reproduction and improvement in the quality of human resources labour is remunerated in accordance with its participation in social activity:

1.  As individuals          - wages and salaries

2.  As members of teams      - bonuses from social,
    of employees               housing and other
                               funds

3.  As members of society    - benefits from common
                               social funds.


## Surplus Determination and Income Distribution

The micro-efficiency of the operations of each
enterprise is measured by value added (surplus) and
residual income.  The motivation system assumes a
close relationship between the rate of growth of
wages and salaries and the rate of growth of
surplus.  In addition, the incentives fund and
standard of living improvement fund are linked
closely to the level of wages and salaries fund.
[7]
        The premium fund for top management as a form
of incentive, depends on the increase in the
efficiency of the enterprise as reflected in
residual income.
        The predetermined gross income is calculated
so as to cover all payments to the government
budget and provide the budgeted residual income.
New product prices can, however, cover some extra
margin to stimulate innovations.
        The initial prices for manufacturing
enterprises are required to be constructed in such
a way as to cover all socially necessary costs.
Generally speaking, standard prices are based on
the average standard branch cost plus gross profit.
        The standard sales prices for manufacturing
enterprises are adjusted to current conditions in
the domestic market through special sales taxes.
        Revenues from sales are recognised in the
accounting period in which they are realised, (i.e.
when goods are shipped or services are rendered to
the customer).  By matching the revenues from sales
with the cost of goods sold there is obtained the
gross income from operation of the enterprise by
using the accrual concept of accounting.  The cost
of goods sold embraces general and administrative
costs as well as sales expenses.
        Tax related to the state fund for fixed
assets - the amount transferred to government
budget as a form of payment for using national
resources and forcing the enterprise to utilise

fixed assets with at least minimum efficiency.

Tax related to wages and salaries - an amount equal to a fixed rate of wages and salaries is paid into the government budget for the common social fund so as to stimulate labour productivity.

Government subsidies for unprofitable goods - increase revenues of the enterprise to compensate for prices set below the manufacturing cost of product. Residual income is adjusted by state authorised public accountants in respect of windfall profits and irregular profits. These are deducted from residual income. Independent profits arise from changes in prices, and tariffs. Windfall profits arise from government decisions and are transferred to the government budget. Irregular profits occur when enterprises exhibit anti-social behaviour. For example, product quality lowered in relation to authorised standards, excessive profit obtained from non-typical production as well as unjustified reductions in expenditure on industrial safety, environmental protection etc. [8]

Income tax - taxation of the enterprise's income is arranged in such a way as to satisfy the need for incentives for top management and the development of the enterprise. Income tax is determined by branch ministries as a percentage of average fixed assets (gross book value) and inventories. Any increase in post-tax profits over the preceding year is subject to progressive taxation.

## Concluding Remarks

Micro-accounting deals, as we can see, with efficiency measurement, understood as a conversion of what is to some extent a given input into largely controlled output. Step by step, following the greater degree of freedom of decision making, the efficiency of a micro-economic unit seems to be closer and closer to the real effectiveness that can be measured at present rather at the macro-economic level (gross national product, national income, value added).

In Poland uniform accounting has been developed to enable a rational allocation of resources within the entire economy and control of plan fulfilment. Input-output tables for the entire economy as well as computation of gross national product and national income and their

distribution are based on standardised accounting,
[9]. The need for macro-economic accounting
information is one of the basic arguments for the
standardisation of accounting on the basis of a
well established accounting theory [10].


NOTES AND REFERENCES

1. Private farms contribute 81.5 per cent of
total agricultural output - see Pawel Bozyk, The
Economy in Poland, (Interpress, 1975).
    The state-owned units constitute the majority
of all units (they generate 71.6 per cent of national income in Poland). For co-operative units and
private ones percentage rates are respectively 8.9
and 19.5 (see Statistical Year Book, Warsaw, 1975,
p.44).
2. Pawel Bozyk, The Economy in Poland,
(Interpress, 1975).
3. A. Wakar, Morfologia bodzcow
ekonomicznych, (Morphology of Incentives), (PWE,
Warszawa, 1968).
    From his school's economic point of view the
three-part formula 'prices - accounting -
incentives' functions in different ways in terms of
strictly planned economy and in the economy using
both planning system and market mechanism.
4. On the present stage of the world economy
see Kornai J., Anti-Equilibrium, Amsterdam, North
Holland Publish. Co., 1971, Theorem 23.1.
5. See O. Lange, Ekonomia Polityczna,
(Political Economics), (PWN, Warsaw), 1955.
6. See B. Glinski, Economy Functioning,
PWE, Warszawa, 1977.
7. See A. Jaruga, Z. Jaglinska, Social
Accounting in Poland - State of the Art. Paper
presented at the Workshop on Comparative European
Accounting, Amsterdam, November, 1977.
8. See A. Jaruga, Some Developments of
Auditing in Poland, The International Journal of
Accounting, Vol.12, No.1, 1976, pp.101-109.
9. See A. Jaruga, Problems of uniform
accounting principles in Poland, The International
Journal of Accounting, Vol.8, No.1, 1972, pp.25-51.
10. See T. Peche, Podstawy wspolczesnej
ewidencji gospodarczej, (Fundamentals of Modern
Business Recording), (PWN, Warszawa, 1973).

Chapter Nine

## ACCOUNTING IN THE USSR

Derek Bailey

Economic System

In the USSR the means of production and natural
resources are in state ownership.  Acting under
directives from the Politburo of the Central
Committee of the Communist Party of the Soviet
Union the State Planning Commission prepares a
national plan for economic and social development.
In the plan there is established the direction and
pace of economic development, the composition and
volume of output, the relative rates of expansion
of different industries and the capital investment
programme.  Thus, strategic planning is
centralised.
        The implementation of the national economic
plan is the responsibility of the industrial
ministries and other agencies controlling and
directing the work of the enterprises, all of which
are in state ownership.
        The national economic plan is disaggregated to
the industrial ministries and, ultimately, to
enterprises.  In principal the corporate plan
(tekhpromfinplan) of the enterprises is a component
of the national economic plan.
        For the implementation of the plan resources
are allocated to the enterprises by the central
authorities.  Generally, there is no direction of
labour to specific places of work.  The system of
remuneration is intended to ensure an apropriate
distribution of labour among different industries
and tasks.  The rates of pay are determined by the
State Committee on Labour and Wages.  The State
Committee on Prices is responsible for setting
prices throughout the economy.
        Enterprises deliver finished products into the

wholesale network at approved prices. Products
pass into the retail outlets, and so to consumers,
at authorised prices. Retail prices are set so as
to clear the planned supply of consumer goods. The
aggregated remuneration is planned to match the
retail value of the products made available to
consumers.

The primary task of the enterprise is the
conversion of the allocation of resources into the
designated outputs. The director of an enterprise
is confronted by the technical problems of the
production processes rather than by the commercial
problem of the marketplace. From the industrial
ministries instructions flow down to the
enterprises and data on performance against the
plan flows in the reverse direction.

There are problems in designing a motivation
system that will stimulate personnel to operate the
enterprises efficiently. There are also problems
in the selection and utilisation of indicators for
the evaluation of enterprise performance.

Short-term and medium-term finance is provided
by the State Bank. All the monetary transactions
of enterprises are cleared through the State Bank
so that it can monitor their activities. Most of
these transactions are performed by adjusting the
balances in the accounts of the affected
organisations held at the State Bank. The release
of monies for the payment of wages and salaries is
controlled by the same institution.


Accounting System

In the USSR accounting has been converted into an
instrument of national economic administration.
The development of centrally directed social
production has made necessary economic data
processing (khozyaistvennyi uchet) that 'reflects
the process of extended socialist reproduction and
is an instrument for the planned direction of the
national economy'. [1]

More specifically, socialist economic data
processing has been described as:

'a system for the observance, measurement,
registration, processing and transmission of
information on the occurrence of economic
activities necessary for the management of
social production'. [2]

In reality there are three systems:

Statistical data processing (statisticheskii uchet)

accounting data processing (bukhgalterskii uchet)

operational data processing (operativnyi uchet)

Both statistical data processing and accounting data processing are countrywide systems, manually or otherwise conducted, for the collection, classification, summarisation and transmission of data relating to enterprise performance to the superior authorities. The former system also handles more general economic and social data. Operational data processing refers to the less formal recording systems developed within enterprises to service the daily operational needs of particular managers.

Ultimate responsibility for the operation of the statistical and accounting data processing systems rests with the Council of Ministers. Under the Constitution of the USSR the Council of Ministers is empowered:

'... to organise ... a uniform system of accounting and statistics (uchet i statistika) ...' [3]

The overall direction of these two systems is realised by the Central Statistical Administration (TsSU). The responsibility for accounting methodology is entrusted to the Ministry of Finance but exercised in collaboration with the TsSU.

The all-union chart of accounts, systems of accounting records (e.g. the journal voucher system) [4] and the format of the periodical accounting returns are agreed between the Ministry of Finance and the Central Statistical Administration (TsSU). The basic instructions concerning production expenditure accounting and output cost determination are agreed between the Ministry of Finance, the State Planning Commission and the TsSU. The Ministry of Finance is responsible for the operation of the standardised accounting data processing system throughout the national economy. Within the Ministry responsibility devolves upon:

| | |
|---|---|
| Accounting and Reporting Administration | for implementation |
| Control and Audit Administration | for audit and investigations |

Attached to the Ministry of Finance is the Finance Scientific Research Institute, recently involved in the revision of the national chart of accounts, and the Finansy Publishing House.

In the operation of the accounting system the Ministry of Finance is advised by its Accounting and Reporting Methodological Council containing specialists from industry, educational and research institutions.

Within each industrial ministry, and for the enterprises under its control, responsibility for the operation of the standardised accounting system devolves upon its accounting and reporting administration. Its head (nachal'nik), effectively a chief accountant, may be advised by a methodological council. Within the general framework of the standardised accounting system, and the regulations and instructions received from superior authorities, each industrial ministry may issue supplementary directions for the operation of the accounting systems in its subordinate enterprises.

The standardised accounting system is both universal and obligatory in its application and embraces:

- national chart of accounts

- authorised procedures for the recording, classification and summarisation of data in the accounting records

- approved systems of accounting records

- standard forms for the periodical accounting returns.

Thus, the standardised accounting system incorporates the specification of the procedures for the complete cycle of accounting from the initial recording of the events for which accounting is required, the classification and summarisation of these events through the accounting records to the compilation of the periodical accounting returns.

The principal legislative instruments governing accounting are:

- Regulation on Accounting Returns and Balance Sheets, approved by the Council of Ministers on 29 June 1979

- Regulation on Chief Bookkeepers, approved by the Council of Ministers on 24 January 1980

- Regulation on Documents and Records for Accounting in Enterprises and Economic Organisations, approved by the Council of Ministers on 18 October 1961.

The Soviet accounting system is intended to provide an evidential record, corroborated by documentation, of the activities of the enterprise. That is, the system is required to provide 'a complete (i.e. continuous and comprehensive) reflection of all economic operations'. [5] The periods of time for which the various accounting records are required to be preserved are established by the Main Board for Archives of the Council of Ministers. For example, retention periods have been specified as follows:

| Balance sheets - monthly | for one year |
|---|---|
| Balance sheets - quarterly | for three years |
| Balance sheets - annual | for ten years |

The prime function of Soviet accounting has been the realisation of control (kontrol') for the implementation of the plans, the economical use of resources in the attainment of the planned objectives and the protection of socialist property. In its Soviet meaning the term control signifies both validation and verification, such as for the actual existence of tangible assets or the operating performance attained. The state control function of Soviet accounting stems from the precepts of Lenin, the founder of the Soviet state: 'without a period of socialist accounting and control it would be impossible to reach the lowest rung of communism'. [6]

The accounting control over the implementation of the plans is not confined to the determination of the monetary values of realised output, costs incurred, profit achieved and the entitlement to profit-related bonus awards. Accounting control has been accorded a wider scope. For example:

'accounting for wages makes possible control for
the amount of labour and the extent of consumption
and reveals the relationship between the rates of
growth of labour productivity and the average
wage'. [7] Common concepts are employed for the
purposes of planning and accounting.

Over many decades the principal thrust in the
development of the Soviet accounting system has
been in the direction of the increasing
standardisation and simplification of the
accounting procedures. The implementation of the
state control function makes necessary the
operation of the Soviet accounting system with a
tolerable degree of reliability in all enterprises
throughout the USSR, irrespective of the quality
and the changing composition of the accounting
personnel. For this reason there has been a
continuous attempt to standardise and simplify to
the greatest possible extent the accounting
procedures. By this means the implementation of
the control function has been made easier, a
smaller proportion of the available skilled
personnel absorbed into accounting work,
instruction in the operation of the system
simplified and there has been made possible a more
effective audit. On the other hand, the reduction
of accounting to routinely performed clerical
bookkeeping procedures has retarded accounting
development and stultified accounting thought.


## Chief Bookkeeper

The chief bookkeeper (glavnyi bukhgalter) of the
Soviet industrial undertaking may be described as a
comptroller and bears a dual responsibility. For
administrative matters he is responsible to the
chief executive of the undertaking (i.e. director
of an enterprise or the director-general of a
multi-plant combine or ob''edinenie). For matters
concerning the organisation of accounting,
compilation of the accounting returns and the
methods used in the implementation of control the
chief bookkeeper is responsible to the equivalent
official at the next higher level of administration
within the industrial ministry. Ultimate
responsibility for accounting matters rests with
the Ministry of Finance.

The chief bookkeeper is responsible for:

- implementation of the accounting system

Accounting in the USSR

- production expenditure accounting

- output cost determination

- compilation of the accounting returns

- correct calculation and prompt transfer of sums
  to the state budget (e.g. in respect of profits
  and for social insurance), to the banks (e.g.
  for repayment of credits) and to fund accounts
  (e.g. to provide for bonus awards).

In exercising the function of state controller
the chief bookkeeper is required:

- to sign all documents for the receipt and
  dispatch of monies, goods and other valuables

- to sign all documents affecting the credit and
  payment obligations of the undertaking

- to review contracts for the provision of goods
  and services

- to review orders (prikazy) for the
  establishment of posts, the fixing of salaries
  and the setting up of incentive schemes

- to sign all accounting returns and balance
  sheets and certain statistical returns.

The chief bookkeeper is required to ensure
that the resources at the disposal of the
enterprise are used for authorised purposes and
that the approved prices and rates are observed.
Violations of the regulations and illegal acts by
members of the enterprise are required to be
reported to the appropriate authorities by the
chief bookkeeper.
The duty of surveillance over the activities
of the enterprise inevitably leads to a measure of
tension between the accounting personnel and the
other personnel of the enterprise.

Accounting Department

The accounting department is managed by the chief
bookkeeper. It is required to be organised as a
distinct and separate function of administration
within the enterprise. The accounting department

139

is organised into a number of sections, the most important being:

| | |
|---|---|
| labour and wages section | – usually the largest section within the accounting department because of the variety and complexity of the methods for the calculation of remuneration according to the work performed |
| material values section | – accounting for all labour embodied values such as raw materials, finished products, production tools and appliances, basic means of production |
| cost accounting section | – production expenditure accounting and output cost determination |
| general section | – maintenance of the general ledger and the compilation of the accounting returns |
| finance section | – accounts settlement and accounting for monetary resources. |

In the larger industrial undertakings the finance section may be replaced by a separate finance department headed by a treasurer (finansist). Usually the treasurer is subordinated to the chief economist and not to the chief bookkeeper. The post of chief economist with responsibility for the economic planning departments was introduced into enterprises during the nineteen-sixties.

The work of the accounting department is restricted to retrospective accounting. That is, the work of the accounting personnel comprises the maintenance of the accounting records for the activities undertaken by the enterprise, the compilation therefrom of the periodical accounting returns and, to some extent, the analysis of the contents of the latter. At the same time the chief bookkeeper is forbidden to provide unsolicited accounting information to superior authorities.

For the better organisation of the work of the accounting department the chief bookkeeper prepares an annual workplan containing sections dealing with:

i)     documentation and paperwork flow

ii)    procedure for conduct of stocktaking

iii)   control accounts and subsidiary accounts to be opened and the accounts to be used in the recording of specific transactions

iv)    accounting records to be maintained

v)     accounting returns to be compiled.


## Accounts Compilation

At the beginning of 1986 a revised chart of accounts was introduced. It is structured as follows:

|  | Account class | Number of control accounts |
|---|---|---|
| i) | Basic means | 3 |
| ii) | Production stocks | 11 |
| iii) | Production expenditures | 12 |
| iv) | Finished output, commodities and realisation | 14 |
| v) | Monetary resources | 5 |
| vi) | Current accounts | 15 |
| vii) | Financial results and utilisation of profits | 5 |
| viii) | Funds and reserves | 5 |
| ix) | Bank credit and other finance | 7 |

The control accounts are identified by a two digit code although the decimal system of coding is not employed.

The national chart of accounts also contains five memorandum accounts. The single entry memorandum accounts are identified by a three digit code and used principally for recording items in the possession of the enterprise but not at its disposal (e.g. hired equipment).

The national chart of accounts is designed for

application in industrial, agricultural, construction, trade and transportation undertakings as well as other organisations engaged in economic activities.

Within the enterprises subordinated to particular industrial ministries subsidiary ledger accounts may be opened to accord with their needs.

Although some enterprises are subsidised from the state budget the majority of enterprises are expected to recoup their operating expenses from the revenues derived from the provision of products and services. That is, economically responsible behaviour is expected of the management of Soviet enterprises. Economic responsibility (khozraschet) may be described as a method for the planned administration of socialist economic entities and comprises:

- combination of centralised planned direction of the national economy with operational autonomy for each economic entity

- acceptance of responsibility for the fulfilment of economic plans at each level of industrial administration

- assignment of basic means and circulating means to each economic entity

- recoupment of expenditure out of income and the provision of a profit by each economic entity

- combination of the personal material interest of every worker with the general interest of society

- rouble control by the state over the activities of economic entities.

The economically responsible enterprise is required not only to fulfil its economic plan but also to generate a surplus sufficient to provide for the replenishment of its economic stimulation funds and for the appropriation of a portion of the profit to the state budget.

Rouble control (kontrol' rublem), or control over the monetary flows across the boundary of the economic entity, is required to be complemented by a regime of economical housekeeping (rezhim ekonomii) within the economic entities. The latter is reinforced by the concept of materially responsible person (material'no otvetstvennoe litso). That is, the responsible officials entrusted with material, commodities and monetary resources, such as storekeepers and cashiers, may be surcharged with the cost of shortages and damages incurred.

There is a two-fold classification of expenditures. The outgoings of the enterprise are classified by expenditure elements (elementy zatrat) for the purpose of production expenditure accounting (uchet zatrat na proizvodstvo). There is a complementary classification by cost items (stat'i kal'kulyatsii) for the purpose of output cost determination (kal'kulyatsiya sebestoimosti produktsii).

The inputs to the enterprise are classified by expenditure elements:

raw and basic processed materials
auxiliary materials
fuel
power
basic and supplementary wages
social insurance contributions
amortisation
other expenses.

This classification is used in the calculation of the national income created in industry.

The outlays attributed to outputs are classified by cost items:

raw and basic processed materials
fuel and power used for technological purposes
basic wages of production workers
supplementary wages of production workers
social insurance contributions
starting-up and assimilation of production
  expenses
maintenance and utilisation of equipment expenses
shops expenses
works expenses
spoilt output
other production expenses
non-production expenses.

The classification by cost items is used in the accumulation of costs for the determination of production cost (fabrichno-zavodskaya sebestoimost') and the total cost of output (polnaya sebestoimost').

Accrual accounting based on historic costs is employed for the determination of total cost (i.e. embracing both direct costs and indirect costs). Variable costs and fixed costs are not distinguished in the accounting records. There is some use of predetermined costs (i.e. normativnaya sebestoimost' or normative cost) for the purposes of both product cost control and product cost determination (i.e. actual product cost = normative cost + apportionment of cost variances). The accounting tool of normative cost (specific to a particular enterprise) ought not to be confused with the planning tool of planned cost (usually related to the average costs for a number of enterprises). Standard costing is not used for the managerial control of the incidence of cost. Hitherto direct costing has not been employed. The Soviet practice of one-man management (edinonachalie or, practically, managerial autocracy) has probably been an effective obstacle to the development of systems of managerial cost control.

The total cost of output is offset against realised sales income in the Realisation account. The balance on the account, representing the profit on realisation, is transferred to the Profits and Losses account. Into the latter account are carried extraordinary and non-recurring gains and losses such as:

losses arising from natural disasters (e.g. spring floods)

irrecoverable debts

profit/loss from housing and communal services division.

The resulting balance represents the net profit (chistaya pribyl').

The proposed utilisation of profits is set out in the annual financial plan (i.e. balans dokhodov i raskhodov or income and expenditure balance). The utilisation of profits is governed by regulations such as Regulation on the Procedure for the Distribution of Profits approved by the Ministry of Finance, the State Planning Commission and the State Bank on 12 April 1967.

During the course of the year interim appropriations of profit are made for such purposes as:

- payment for the use of basic funds and circulating funds

- transfers to the economic stimulation funds:

  material incentives fund

  socio-cultural activities and housing construction fund

  production development fund

- payment of bank interest.

The amounts appropriated to the state budget are withdrawn in nine equal instalments during the course of each quarter.  The interim appropriations of profit are recorded in the Withdrawn Resources on Account of Profits account.

The final appropriation of profits is determined upon the ratification of the annual balance sheet and the annual report of the enterprise.  The profits are appropriated in the following sequence:

- primary appropriations

  payment for the use of basic funds and circulating funds

  fixed (rental) payment

  bank interest

- secondary appropriations

  transfers to the economic stimulation funds

- tertiary appropriations

  for various purposes such as:

    contribution to the financing of centralised capital investment

    contribution to the financial assistance reserve of the industrial ministry

    contribution to the scientific and technological development fund of the industrial ministry

145

repayment of bank credits for capital investment provided to the enterprise

expansion of the owned circulating means of the enterprise

defraying expenses of cultural and training institutions and pioneer camps operated by the enterprise

reimbursing losses incurred by housing and communal services division of the enterprise.

The fixed (rental) payment is intended to cream off for the state budget profits attributable to especially favourable natural or technical conditions. The balance of otherwise unappropriated profits (svobodnyi ostatok pribyli) is transferred to the state budget.
So as to lessen the arbitrary nature of profits appropriation, and to provide an improved stimulus to the personnel of the enterprise, in 1979 there was introduced the standard method of profits appropriation (normativnyi metod raspredeleniya pribyli). For the more profitable enterprises the rates of deduction for the major appropriations are stabilised for the duration of the five year planning period.
There is a common format to the balance sheet for all industrial enterprises. The format may be summarised as follows:

| | | | |
|---|---|---|---|
| I | Basic means and non-circulating means | I | Sources of owned and equivalent means |
| II | Normed circulating means | II | Bank credits against normed circulating means |
| III | Monetary resources, debtors and other assets | III | Miscellaneous bank credits, creditors and other liabilities |
| IV | Resources and expenditures of capital construction | IV | Sources of resources for capital construction |
| V | Expenditure on formation of basic herd | V | Finance for formation of basic herd |

The balance sheet is compiled for the first of each month. For each of the five subdivisions of the balance sheet sub-totals are provided in addition to the grand totals. In effect, five pairs of sources and applications of funds are aligned in the balance sheet. For each item there are shown the figures for the start of the year and as at the date of the balance sheet. For the normed circulating means (i.e. production stocks and unrealised deliveries) there are shown also the norm values for the start of the year and as at the date of the balance sheet.

The basic means (i.e. labour embodied fixed assets exclusive of natural resources) are shown on the balance sheet at the value notified at the time of acquisition. The accumulated depreciation is shown on the opposite side of the balance sheet. Both depreciation (iznos) and amortisation (amortizatsiya) [8] are shown in the accounts at the rates authorised by resolution (postanvlenie) of the Council of Ministers. Materials, work-in-progress and finished products are shown at actual cost. Unrealised deliveries are shown at total cost.

It is not possible to compile the balance sheet directly from the balances shown in the control accounts. Instead it is necessary to search through the accounting records for the relevant figures. In excess of one hundred items are shown on the balance sheet. In preparation for the compilation of the year-end balance sheet the enterprise is required during October to December (i.e. depending upon the climate) to undertake an inventory of its assets. The balance sheet is signed by the chief executive and the chief bookkeeper.

The major annual accounting returns, apart from the year-end balance sheet, are:

F.3      Movement on the state fund
F.4sp    Deficiencies, misappropriation and damage
         of commodity and material values
F.5      Production expenditures
F.6      Cost of commodity output
F.6 appendix  Digest of the profitability of the
              most important types of output
F.7      Production servicing and management
         expenses
F.8      Report on fulfilment of output plan
F.9      Report on fulfilment of labour plan

F.10   Movement of means of financing and special
       funds
F.11   Report on presence and movement of basic
       funds and amortisation fund
F.12   Realisation of output
F.20   Profits and losses

The range and format of the accounting returns
are determined by the Ministry of Finance in
conjunction with the Central Statistical
Administration.
On the basis of the accounting returns the
chief executive is answerable to the higher Party
and state authorities.
The balance sheet and accounting returns for
the enterprise are presented to:

- next higher level of administration within the
  industrial ministry

- branch of the State Bank holding the bank
  accounts of the enterprise

- branch of the Construction Bank providing
  credit facilities

- local office of the Central Statistical
  Administration

- local office of the Ministry of Finance.

The monthly balance sheet is required to be
submitted within twelve days of the end of the
month.  The year-end balance sheet and the annual
accounting returns are required to be presented by
25th January of the following year.
The accounting returns are intended to provide
a system of interrelated indicators revealing:

- composition of the resources at the disposal of
  the enterprise

- utilisation of basic means and circulating
  means

- plan performance

- results of economic activities.

The system of indicators incorporated into the
accounting returns is constructed on the basis of
148

the indicators stipulated in the corporate plan
(tekhpromfinplan or technical, industrial and
financial plan) of the enterprise.
    The accounting returns are used by:

  - the higher level of industrial administration
    for the evaluation of enterprise performance

  - the banks for monitoring the financial
    situation of the enterprise

  - the local statistical office for processing
    statistical data

  - the local finance office for the collection of
    revenues for the state budget.

    The balance sheet is used to determine:

  - composition and sources for the financing of
    the owned circulating means

  - adequacy of owned circulating means

  - correctness and promptness of financial
    transactions with the state budget

  - correctness and promptness of settlement with
    debtors and creditors

  - correctness of the formation and utilisation of
    the special funds and special purpose finance

  - rate of turnover of circulating means and the
    ways for its improvement.

    The chief executive of the industrial
undertaking is required to prepare an annual report
(ob"yasnitel'naya zapiska or explanatory document).
The annual report contains:

  - an overall assessment of the work of the
    enterprise

  - the measures to be implemented for improving
    performance in the coming year

  - an assessment of the state of planning and
    accounting.

    The annual report provides an appraisal of

performance in comparison with the plan and an explanation of any failure to achieve the planned goals. In the annual report there are a number of sections for dealing with such matters as:

- organisational structure

- production capacity

- innovation and rationalisation

- material and technical supply

- labour and wages

- industrial safety

- training

- capital construction.

Within the enterprise there may be convened a meeting or series of meetings of the workforce or, more usually, of Party and other activists to consider the annual report with particular reference to:

- results of the year's activities

- measures projected for the coming year.

The management board (glavnoe upravlenie) of an industrial ministry is required to examine systematically the accounting returns and reports for its subordinate enterprises and to adopt measures for the improvement of their work. The local offices of the State Bank, Construction Bank, Central Statistical Administration and the Ministry of Finance may participate in these examinations and the ensuing deliberations. These authorities have the right:

- to demand explanations of the data contained in the accounting returns

- to examine accounting and other documents and the entries in the accounting records

- to examine the materials relating to audit (reviziya) and inspection (obsledovanie).

The management board is required to secure the agreement of the financial authorities to its decisions.  In the event of disagreement the representatives for the State Bank, Construction Bank or the Ministry of Finance may refer the matter for resolution to the council of ministers of the relevant union republic.

At the conclusion of the deliberations decisions are taken on:

- appropriation of profits for the preceding year

- determination of the sources for the recoupment of losses

- reprimands for past shortcomings in performance

- recommendations for the improvement of performance

- correction of errors uncovered in the accounting returns.

It is at this stage that there is undertaken the reformation (reformirovanie) of the balance sheet to reflect the decisions on the appropriation of profits.  The decisions taken are notified to the interested authorities.  The management board is required to ratify the annual report and notify its decisions to the enterprise within fifteen days of the report's receipt.

The accounting returns prepared by the higher levels of industrial administration (i.e. management board and industrial ministry) are similar in format to those authorised for the subordinate enterprises.  These accounting returns summarise:

- work of subordinate enterprises

- financial transactions undertaken.

The quarterly and annual accounting returns prepared by the management board are submitted to:

- industrial ministry

- Ministry of Finance

- Central Statistical Administration

- Board of the State Bank

- Board of the Construction Bank.

The industrial ministry is required to ratify the annual accounting returns within twenty days of their receipt. For decisions taken with respect to these accounting returns the industrial ministry is required to notify the Ministry of Finance and the State Bank in addition to the management board.

The summarised accounting returns of the industrial ministry are presented to:

- State Planning Commission

- Ministry of Finance

- Central Statistical Administration.

The quarterly accounting returns prepared by the industrial ministry are required to be submitted within forty days of the end of the quarter and the annual accounting returns, by 1st April of the following year. The annual accounting returns are presented also to the Council of Ministers.

The industrial ministries are required to provide supplementary accounting returns dealing with:

- balance of income and expenditure

- composition and utilisation of the financial assistance reserve

- basic means and capital repairs expenditure

- provision of bonuses for the fulfilment of important tasks and extraordinary financial assistance to workers

- number of personnel and wages paid.

Both management boards and industrial ministries are expected to prepare annual reports dealing with:

- principal factors affecting the work of subordinate enterprises

- measures to be implemented for:

    output cost reduction

    increasing profitability

    improving utilisation of basic means and
    circulating means

    improving financial position of the industry.

The upward flow of accounting returns is
complemented by a flow of statistical returns.  The
latter are processed through the all-union network
of local statistical offices attached to the
Central Statistical Administration.  In this manner
summarised data is produced for:

- branches of industry

- economic regions

- union republics

- national economy.

The Central Statistical Administration
presents summarised statistical returns to the
Council of Ministers, the State Planning
Commission, the Ministry of Finance and the Board
of the State Bank.  These statistical returns are
used for:

- monitoring the implementation of the national
  economic plan

- determination of the social product and the
  national income

- compilation of the balance of the national
  economy

- studying the structure and distribution of the
  labour resources

- planning the productivity of social labour.

## Accounting Development

Soviet accounting developed as a data processing

153

tool to service the need for the centralised
administration of a state controlled economy.
Accounting was confined to the fulfilment of a
state control function. To ensure the effective
operation of the Soviet system of accounting, and
to lessen its labour power requirement, emphasis
was placed upon the standardisation and
simplification of accounting procedures. The
transition from manual accounting systems to punched
card accounting and, more recently, the gradual
extension of computer operation to accounting has
led to the centralisation of accounting services
(e.g. the creation of accounting bureaux serving a
number of enterprises). These developments have
rendered the Soviet accounting system increasingly
less capable of responding to local rquirements for
accounting information.
    Since the nineteen-sixties there have been
intermittent attempts to realise a measure of
economic reform through the decentralisation of
some economic decision-making power. A consequence
has been the emergence of a potential need for
accounting information within the industrial
undertaking. During these two decades there has
been an expansion of the more-or-less informal and
localised operational data processing procedures.
    At the October 1978 meeting of the
methodological council of the Accounting and
Reporting Administration of the Ministry of Finance
A.S. Narinskii, a leading specialist at the Finance
and Economics Institute in Leningrad, gave an
address on prospective measures for the
improvement of accounting in industrial
undertakings. [9] He indicated the need for a
radical reconstruction (korennaya perestroika) of
Soviet accounting. At the succeeding meeting of
the methodological council in January 1979 two
commissions were established. [10] The commissions
were entrusted with the task of formulating
proposals for the improvement of accounting.
    In 1982 V.F. Palii, a leading specialist
attached to the Avtozil motor vehicle undertaking,
acknowledged that the importance of the information
function had not been recognised and its place
within the Soviet system of accounting had not been
determined. [11]
    At a major accounting conference held in May
1986 in Donetsk there was issued a call for the
reconstruction of both the accounting personnel and
the accounting system. The accounting personnel
were exhorted 'not to be merely registrars of

economic operations'. [12]

What do Soviet specialists mean by the expression 'the reconstruction of accounting'?

Narinskii argued that the first stage of accounting reconstruction should be directed to the 'localisation of expenditure' so as to expand the frontier of direct accounting (pryamyi uchet). Since that time there has been a steady expansion in the attribution of the expenditures incurred by the industrial undertaking to expense centres. A new term has entered the Soviet accounting vocabulary: expense centre (mesto zatrat). Initially the expense centres were conceived merely as physical locations. At the Donetsk conference for the first time some speakers emphasised the desirability of accounting by responsibility centres (tsentr otvetstvennosti).

At the same conference N.G. Chumachenko, a distinguished Ukrainian accounting specialist, called for experiments in direct costing (direkt-kosting) to be undertaken by some of the industrial ministries. Another speaker suggested that the experiments be conducted in the light and foodstuffs industries. The adoption of direct costing would be advantageous if enterprises were to be encouraged 'to strive for the product assortment most beneficial and economically efficient from the point of view of net output and profit' as has been suggested by the pricing specialist A. Komin. [13]

M. Gorbachev, the general secretary of the Communist Party of the Soviet Union, has popularised the concepts of reconstruction (perestroika) and openness (glasnost') and advocated their application to all aspects of Soviet economic and social life. In his address to the XXVII Congress of the CPSU, held in February 1985 in Moscow, Gorbachev set the task of 'the most thorough reorganisation of the socialist economic mechanism'. [14] The prospective reorganisation, or reconstruction, of the economic mechanism has implications for the practice of accounting. There will emerge new needs for accounting information requiring an appropriate adaptation, or reconstruction, of the Soviet system of accounting. The recognition of the information function may be regarded as the extension of openness to accounting. The leading Soviet accounting specialists are attuned to the possibilities and opportunities arising in the newly unfolding situation. On the other hand, the response of the gnerality of accounting workers may well be sluggish and wayward. [15]

REFERENCES

1. Kostyuk, P.A., Slovar' Bukhgaltera (Minsk, 1984), p.212.
2. Palii, V.F. and Ya. V. Sokolov, Teoriya bukhgalterskogo ucheta (Moscow 1984), p.6.
3. Konstitutsiya (Osnovnoi Zakon) SSSR (Moscow, 1977).
4. Berry, M., Accounting in Socialist Countries in H.P. Holzer et al, International Accounting (Harper & Row, 1984), p.421.
5. Palii, V.F. and Ya. V. Sokolov, op. cit, p.30.
6. Lenin, V.I., Polnoe sobranie sochinenii, Vol.44, pp.157-158.
7. Palii, V.F. and Ya. V. Sokolov, loc. cit.
8. Bailey, D.T., Accounting for the Depreciation of Plant and Machinery in the Soviet Enterprise, Accountant's Magazine, April, 1974, pp.111-116.
9. Bukhgalterskii uchet, 1978, No.I, pp.39-42 and 63. See Soviet and East European Acounting Bulletin, 1980, No.3, pp.89-107.
10. Bukhgalterskii uchet, 1979, No.5, pp.58-63.
11. Bukhgalterskii uchet, 1982, No.11, pp.50-51.
12. Bukhgalterskii uchet, 1986, No.8, pp.7-8 and pp.50-54.
13. Planovoe khozyaistvo, 1986, No.5, pp.59-65.
14. Gorbachev, M., Political Report of the CPSU Central Committee to the 27th Party Congress, (Novosti, Moscow, 1986), p.43.
15. Bailey, D.T., Soviet Accounting - Under Reconstruction, Management Accounting (UK), June 1987, pp.16-23.

Chapter Ten

## ACCOUNTING IN YUGOSLAVIA

Ivan Turk

## Introduction

Accounting is a function of a given socio-economic
system and from the accounting theory appropriate
to that system flows the accounting practice.  This
chapter presents the general features of accounting
in Yugoslav enterprises and makes no claim to being
an exhaustive exposition.

The code of accounting principles adopted by
the Yugoslav professional organisation during 1972
and 1973 provided a definition of accounting:
'Accounting embraces the systematised aggregation
of double-entry accounting, budgeting, accounting
control and accounting analysis'.

For planning reports, accounting information
is derived from the budgets, whereas for
achievement reports the accounting information is
derived from the double-entry accounting records.
Both the planning reports and the achievement
reports may be related to a wider or a narrower
area of business activity but in all instances
methodological uniformity in their compilation must
be ensured so as to make possible comparisons.

The essence of accounting analysis lies in the
elucidation of the variances between the planning
reports and the achievement reports and the
determination of their courses.  Budgeting, as an
aspect of accounting, does not represent the
totality of the information connected with planning
and accounting analysis does not represent the full
extent of the analysis of performance needed.
Therefore, the aspects of accounting described as
budgeting and accounting analysis are excluded from
the work of the accounting department and included
in the work of the planning and analytical
department.

157

For the provision of a satisfactory service of accounting information the accounting department should be separated from and be independent of the personnel engaged in the basic business functions of production and selling. To this end there should be a separation of the accounting function from the finance function and of the accounting department from the finance department. But in practice - and despite the wholly dissimilar nature of the task performed - the departments are often combined.

The resources representing each enterprise are owned by society. During the past five years each enterprise has been transformed into an organisation of workers and designated a work organisation (WO). Consequently, the Yugoslav constitution refers to the pooling of labour and resources. The work organisation is the tangible result of such a pooling of labour and resources. Work organisations are not set up as corporations financed by state capital and controlling socially owned resources but primarily as autonomous and self-managing organisations of workers (i.e. in their capacity of employed persons and not as citizens).

Thus the work organisation is an independent self-management of workers united by a common interest in their joint labour and on the basis of socially owned resources. The workers decide on the labour to be performed, the working conditions and the remuneration for their labour and therefore on business policy.

## Working Entities

The larger work organisations may comprise two or more working entities. The workers within each working entity may form a basic organisation of associated labour (BOAL) provided that (i) the results of their joint labour can be expressed separately in monetary terms either within the work organisation (i.e. by transfer prices) or on the market and (ii) the workers can jointly and on terms of equality manage the affairs of their own basic organisation and of the embracing work organisation.

In such an instance the primary socio-economic unit is the BOAL and the WO is represented by the association of a number of basic organisations. In addition the WO may comprise one or more work

158

communities providing administrative, professional
and other services to the BOAL. The accounting
department is included in a work community and
performs accounting work for all the BOALS.

The accounting unit is the primary
socio-economic unit (in effect, a profit centre).
For each BOAL and each work community there is
separate accounting and the preparation of
individual income statements and balance sheets.
For the WO, as an enterprise, there is a
consolidated income statement and balance sheet
(see Diagram 1).

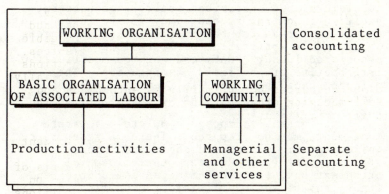

ENTERPRISE

WORKING ORGANISATION — Consolidated accounting

BASIC ORGANISATION OF ASSOCIATED LABOUR

WORKING COMMUNITY

Production activities

Managerial and other services — Separate accounting

Diagram 1

In an organisation of basic labour, accounting
serves the needs of workers, self-management
bodies, business executives and other users and
society generally, as a principal source of
information. Cost accounting and management
accounting are orientated to the internal needs of
the organisation. The external interest in
financial accounting data is satisfied through the
implementation of a uniform scheme of accounts and
a uniform format for the income statements and
balance sheets.

A uniform chart of accounts is applicable to
all basic organisations of associated labour and
work communities, irrespective of their field of
operations. It is applied not only to industrial
and commercial enterprises but also to hospitals,

schools etc. There are separate uniform charts of accounts for (i) banks and other financial organisations, (ii) self-managed communities and the organs of socio-political organisations and societies. However, for the work communities, into which all these organisations are subdivided, the uniform chart of accounts mentioned in the preceding paragraph is employed.

Only the uniform chart of accounts for industrial and commercial enterprises is considered in this article. It comprises 407 control accounts grouped into ten classes, the decimal system of numeration being employed. On the basis of the uniform chart of accounts each accounting unit draws up a more elaborate chart of accounts by subdividing the prescribed control accounts but additional control accounts may not be introduced. A uniform format for the balance sheet and income statement is applicable to all basic units of associated labour (BOAL) and work communities (WO), irrespective of the field of operation. The balance sheet comprises 318 items and the income statement 175 items. These documents are intended for external reporting.

For internal purposes completely separate statements may be prepared. There is a separate uniform scheme of balance sheet and income statement for (i) banks and other financial organisations, (ii) self-managed communities and the organs of socio-political communities and (iii) socio-political organisations and societies.

In Yugoslav accounting the business assets are subdivided into fixed assets, current assets and financial investments. In addition, there are reserve assets and common consumption assets. Reserve assets consist of cash corresponding to the part of equities intended for the recoupment of losses (the reserve fund) and may be used only temporarily for offsetting illiquidity. The common consumption assets consist of housing, recreational buildings and equipment, loans advanced to the workers and monies for such purposes, cash earmarked for recreational, cultural and other expenditure.

Fixed assets are revalued at the end of the year if the relevant current purchase prices are more than 10 per cent greater than the original values shown in the accounting records. The revaluation affects also the equities but not loans received for the purchase of such fixed assets.

Work in progress and stocks of semi-finished

and finished products may be valued at a lower
limit, on the basis of direct material costs or, as
an upper limit, on the basis of average material
costs plus minimal depreciation. Within these two
limits each accounting unit may select its own
valuation method. Personal incomes relating to
work in progress are not treated as a part of the
inventory valuation but as a claim against future
income. On the other hand, no personal incomes
relating to stocks of finished products can remain
not set off against the income (in the sense of
newly created value) for that period.

Although material issues may be priced by any
of the methods of moving average, weighted average,
FIFO and LIFO, the most commonly used is the method
of weighted average. But in no case may the
relevant price exceed the current purchase price or
the cost incurred by newly produced quantities of
the same product or the realisable sales price less
the incremental selling costs.

In the first period after World War II the
Yugoslav enterprises were financed by the direct
investment of specific social resources. There
were no repayment obligations. Later the
enterprises were dependent on bank loans.
Additionally, during the latest period, enterprises
may be financed by joint ventures involving
interested domestic organisations or foreign firms.
The repayment of such investment at the end of the
stipulated period is achieved by retaining part of
the income in the accounting unit. Retained income
makes possible the expansion of the accounting unit
without resorting to bank loans or joint ventures.

The main source for the financing of business
assets is the business fund consisting, in essence,
of retained income designated for business
purposes. In a certain sense, the business fund is
the equity capital of the accounting unit and is
either generated internally or transferred from
another unit but without any repayment obligation
(as was true generally in the first post-war
development period).

Nowadays, newly established enterprises (i.e.
work organisations or basic organisations of
associated labour) commence with no business fund.
Initially, the business assets are financed by the
receipt of loans and the incurring of other
liabilities. Later, if the enterprise is
successful, part of its income may be retained for
the creation of a business fund.

On the other hand, work communities never have

161

a business fund. Their business assets exist
always as a liability against those basic
organisations of associated labour for which the
work communities perform services. Work
communities must return all excess income to the
basic organisation and must not be retained for its
expansion.

Because in each accounting unit the funds and
various kinds of liabilities are grouped into
sources of financing for business assets, reserve
assets and common consumption assets, in
correspondence with the classification of assets,
each balance sheet can be divided into several
sub-balance sheets. Of course, the most important
is the sub-balance sheet for the business assets
and their sources of financing.

Generally speaking, the financial result is
the difference between revenues and expenses.
Yugoslav law does not necessarily allow the sale
value of products and services sold on credit to be
treated as revenue. It is required that such sales
value should be received in cash within 15 days or
within the period specified by the credit
instrument guaranteeing payment. For a bill of
exchange the period must not exceed three months.

If, at the end of the accounting period, these
stipulations have not been fulfilled, the sale
value is not reckoned as revenue. Because all the
costs of goods sold must be charged to the income
statement immediately upon their delivery, there is
created a 100 per cent reserve against all trade
debts not settled in cash within the prescribed
periods. The reserve is liquidated when the debts
are settled.

Any gain from the sale of fixed assets is
excluded from revenue and treated as an increase to
the business fund.

Joint ventures arise when two or more
accounting units jointly provide products or
perform services. The revenue from the sale of
such products or services must be distributed among
the respective accounting units so that each
receives its appropriate share.

The financial revenues of an accounting unit
consist of interest received or the shares in the
joint profit obtained by joint ventures.

The prescribed minimal rates of depreciation
are based on single-shift working and are increased
if more shifts are worked. If the appropriate
minimal rate of depreciation is insufficient, the
accounting unit may apply larger rates

corresponding to the actual lives of the fixed
assets. But the accounting unit is not allowed to
conceal profits by the application of excessive
rates of depreciation.

The principal special feature of Yugoslav
accounting is the manner of segregating expenses in
the income statement for the purpose of income
determination. Certain socio-economic categories
are computed before arriving at the financial
result.

First, there is a category of income in the
sense of newly created value. Income is the
central category for decision-making in conditions
of self-management. Income is computed by
deducting from the sales revenue the material costs
and minimal depreciation attributed to the goods
sold. These items are 'expenses before a
determination of gross income'.

Next, there are deducted 'expenses met from
gross income before the determination of net
income'. Such expenses are:

(a)   taxes on gross income (for the
      satisfaction of general social needs
      within the framework of socio-political
      communities);

(b)   contributions from gross income (for the
      satisfaction of collective needs in the
      spheres of education, science, culture
      etc.);

(c)   contractual and other expenses for
      current business needs met out of gross
      income (interest paid, insurance
      premiums, delivery transport,
      depreciation provided in excess of the
      minimal rate, transfers of resources to
      work communities).

From net income there are subtracted personal
income (i.e. net personal incomes and also taxes on
and contributions from personal incomes) already
paid. The residual net income may be distributed
to the workers as additional personal income or to
the common consumption fund or to the reserve fund
or to the business fund. The part of the net
income distributed to the reserve and business fund
is described as 'accumulation'.

If it is not possible to recoup from revenue
all the expenses (i.e. 'expenses before the

determination of gross incomes', 'expenses before the determination of net income', personal incomes already paid), the difference is a loss. In that case, the taxes on and the contributions from income are decreased or eliminated. Depreciation provided in excess of the minimal rate is eliminated. That is, a loss will lead to the correction of some expenses but not personal incomes already paid. The loss incurred can influence the computations of personal incomes in future if the amount paid previously exceeded the amount guaranteed by law or provided for by social compact.

In the income statements the central role is given to income in the sense of a newly created value while in the statements of the financial position (balance sheets) a distinction is made between business assets and other assets. Business assets constitute fixed assets, current assets and investments. Apart from the business assets there are reserve assets and common consumption assets.

The conceptions embraced by the Yugoslav indicators of efficiency are understood best with the help of a simplified structure of the accounting statements. The statement of financial position (balance sheet) is divided always into a number of substatements within the framework of one statement:

Statement of Financial Position

| Assets | | Equities | |
|---|---|---|---|
| Business assets (fixed and current assets) Unrecouped loss | _____ _____ | Business fund Business obligations | _____ _____ |
| Reserve assets | _____ _____ | Reserve fund | _____ _____ |
| Common consumption assets | _____ _____ | Common consumption funds Obligations for common consumption assets | _____ _____ |

The income statement is divided into a number of distinct substatements:

I   Statement of Determination of Operating Income

| Expenses | | Revenues | |
|---|---|---|---|
| Material costs and minimum depreciation for goods sold Extraordinary expenses Operating income | _____ _____ | Revenues from goods sold Other recurring revenues Extraordinary revenues Operating loss (Material costs and minimum depreciation in excess of revenues) | _____ _____ |

II Statement of Allocation of Operating Income

| Expenses | Income |
|---|---|
| Taxes on income (for satisfaction of general social needs within the framework of socio-political communities) | Operating income |
| | Net loss (Taxes, contributions and obligations in excess of operating income) |
| Contributions from income (for satisfaction of collective needs in the sphere of education, science, culture, etc.) | |
| Contractual and other expenses for current business needs out of income (interest, insurance premiums, transportation costs, depreciation in excess of the minimum, transfers to work communities, etc.) | |
| Net income | |

### III   Statement of Allocation of Net Income

| Expenses | Income |
|---|---|
| Personal incomes (net personal incomes plus taxes on and contributins from personal incomes) | Net income Residual loss (Personal incomes in excess of net income) |
| Addition to consumers' consumption fund | |
| Available for accumulation | |

### IVA Statement of Allocation of Accumulation

| Re-Investment | Accumulation |
|---|---|
| Addition to business fund | Available for accumulation |
| Addition to reserve fund | |

167

IVB   Statement of Recoupment of Losses

| Loss | Recoupment |
|------|-----------|
| Operating loss (material costs and minimum depreciation not recouped from revenues) | Reductions of reserve fund |
| | Subsidies |
| | Temporary reduction of business fund |
| Net loss (taxes on and contribution from income, contractual and other expenses not met from operating income) | Closing unrecouped loss |
| Opening unrecouped loss ‾‾‾ | ‾‾‾ |

The operations of the accounting unit cannot be assessed on the basis of only one indicator. The Associated Labour Act stipulates the following basic indicators:

(a)   gross income per worker;

(b)   gross income divided by the average business asset;

(c)   net income per worker;

(d)   accumulation provided by gross income;

(e)   accumulation provided by net income;

(f)   accumulation divided by average business assets;

(g)   personal incomes plus net income distributed to the common consumption fund per worker;

(h)   net personal income per worker.

Each of these indicators has its specific purpose. For instance, the gross income per worker (a) shows the quality of the decision-making affecting the generation of total income. Up to a point, the indicator could be used to reflect the socio-economic productivity of labour but, because of the influence of changing prices, it is insufficiently reliable.

The gross income divided by the average business assets (b) shows where a higher national income for meeting social needs can be created by additional social resources, whereas it is more difficult to use this indicator to assess the efficiency of the accounting unit as such. The workers can most easily assess the efficiency of their integrating into associated labour by means of the indicator of personal incomes and common consumption fund per worker (g). The capacity for expanded reproduction is clearly represented by the indicator of accumulation divided by average business assets (f).

The indicators stipulated in the Associated Labour Act for internal usage may be supplemented by other indicators. Of these additional indicators, accumulation expressed as a percentage of the business fund is important in that it can be

compared directly with the current interest rate
for bank loans.


## External

So far some features of internal accounting only
have been considered.  In addition, there is
external accounting in the form of the Social
Accountancy Service established under the
constitution and operated on the basis of a special
law.  The Social Accountancy Service is integrated
into the overall system for the social supervision
of operating activities and provides a kind of
external record of the operations of the accounting
units.

The Service is involved in the conduct of the
financial transactions because through it are
passed all the financial flows concerning the
accounting unit.  Therefore it is possible to
exercise prior control over all transactions
involving the transfer of funds.  If there is
insufficient cash in the giro account of the
accounting units the Service ensures that the
liabilities are met in accordance with the priority
sequence prescribed by law.

All accounting units must submit to the
Service periodical (for three, six and nine months)
and year-end (for 12 months) financial statements.
The fiscal year, running from 1 January to 31
December, is uniform for all accounting units.  The
periodical financial statements are submitted to
the Service within one month of the end of the
relevant period and the yearly financial statements
by the end of the following February.

The Service exercises supervision over the
accounting units through the control of the
legality of business operations, especially laying
stress on the settling and payment of taxes and
contributions and the granting of loans.  The
supervisory role comprises a control function
performed within the Service and an inspection
function carried out in the accounting units.

At the present time, with the exception of
joint ventures involving foreign firms, no auditing
is undertaken.  In any case, the Service does not
confirm but only evaluates the yearly financial
statements of the accounting units.  The financial
statements are finalised by the workers' council
when the workers have decided upon the distribution
of income.

The main task of the Service is to prepare impartial analysis and provide information for:

(a)   the accounting unit supplying the original data;

(b)   other accounting units wishing to know the current position and the operating success of some other accounting unit;

(c)   the socio-political communities, self-management communities and the Chamber of Commerce;

so as to be in the position to achieve the targets and implement the economic measures contained in the social development plan.

In Yugoslavia the term 'accounting worker' is applied to all persons working on accounting activities. Similarly, the term 'financial worker' is applied to all persons working on financial activities. There are an estimated 400,000 accounting and financial workers in Yugoslavia, equal to 4.8 per cent of all employed (manual and non-manual) workers.

Throughout Yugoslavia there are local societies for accounting and financial workers embracing 24 per cent of all such workers. In each of the constituent republics of Yugoslavia all the local professional societies together constitute a republican association of accounting and financial workers (or, in an autonomous province, the provincial association of accounting and financial workers). Finally, at the federal level there exists the Yugoslav Association of Accounting and Financial Workers.

Each local society organises a programme of meetings for the discussion of professional topics. The republican associations arrange seminars on current professional problems and annual symposia for the consideration of theoretical problems. In addition, the republican associations act as publishers for professional journals.

The professional codes of the republican associations comprise:

(a)   the Code of Accounting Principles;

(b)   the Code of Ethical Conduct for Accounting Workers;

(c)   the Code of the Principles of Financing;

(d)   the Code of Ethical Conduct for Financial
      Workers.

The first two codes, which have been translated
into English, are now undergoing revision.

As mentioned at the beginning of the article,
only the general features of Yugoslav accounting
have been mentioned. However, it is hoped that
this exposition will be of interest to accounting
specialists in other countries.

PART III

CONCLUSION

Chapter Eleven

**ACCOUNTING UNDER SOCIALISM: AN OVERVIEW**

Derek Bailey

For their political philosophy the socialist states
look to the intellectual heritage bequeathed by
Karl Marx and his collaborator Friedrich Engels.
But Marx and Engels provided few indications of
how a socialist economy might be organised. In the
socialist economy the means of production were to
be held in common by the associated producers and
production conducted according to a plan.
Socialised production would become a practical
possibility:

> 'Only a society which makes it possible
> for its productive forces to dovetail
> harmoniously into each other on the
> basis of one single vast plan can allow
> industry to be distributed over the
> whole country in the way best adapted to
> its own development, and to the
> maintenance and development of the other
> elements of production.' [1]

In the administration of the socialist economy
Engels considered that:

> 'The useful effects of the various
> articles of consumption, compared with
> one another and with the quantities of
> labour required for their production,
> will in the end determine the plan.
> People will be able to manage everything
> very simply...' [2]

In the opinion of Marx the maintenance of
accounting records would become 'more necessary in
collective production than in capitalist
production'. [3] However, the occasional

173

references to accounting made by Marx and Engels
were cast in general terms.  It is not possible to
draw any inferences concerning the form to be
taken by, or the use to be made of, accounting
records in the socialist economy.

Marx and Engels were deeply critical of the
modes of behaviour nurtured in capitalist society.
They objected to 'the icy water of egotistical
calculation' that 'left remaining no other nexus
between man and man than naked self-interest'. [4]

Marx was critical of the motivation for
business enterprise in the capitalist economy:

'... the rate of profit is the motive
power of capitalist production.  Things
are produced only so long as they can be
produced with a profit.' [5]

Although their references are scanty, it could
not be inferred reasonably that Marx and Engels
considered accounting would remain unaffected by
the transformation from a capitalist economy to a
socialist economy.

The attempt to establish a socialist economy
fell to Lenin and the Bolsheviks in 1917 in Russia
following the successful October Revolution.
Lenin visualised:

'the transformation of the whole of the
state economic mechanism into a single
huge machine, into an economic organism
that will work in such a way as to enable
hundreds of millions of people to be
guided by a single plan'. [6]

In other words:

'The whole of society will have become a
single office and a single factory'. [7]

Lenin declared:

'Accounting and control - that is the
main thing required for "arranging" the
smooth working, the correct functioning
of the first phase of communist society'.
[8]

He was of the opinion that:

'The accounting and control necessary for

this have been simplified by capitalism
to the extreme and reduced to the
extraordinarily simple operations - which
any literate person can perform - of
supervising and recording, knowledge of
the four rules of arithmetic, and issuing
appropriate receipts'. [9]

At least during the early years of the Soviet
regime in Russia, Lenin appears to have considered
accounting to be nothing other than a form of
clerical record-keeping.  Any attempt at an
assessment of the significance of these remarks
should recognise the two distinct accounting
traditions that co-existed in Continental Europe.
Double entry accounting was being used by men of
business in the quest for profits.  Cameral
accounting was used in the state administration of
the Austro-Hungarian, German and Russian Empires.
Lenin may well have had in mind the latter
accounting tradition.
     In Soviet Russia there was a brief period,
known as War Communism, during which was attempted
the abolition of money and, necessarily, accounting
in monetary terms.  The attempt to administer the
entire national economy through a system of
physical controls led to economic dislocation and a
dramatic fall in industrial efficiency.  The
experiment was abandoned.
     In April 1921 the introduction of the New
Economic Policy marked the restoration of money and
the establishment of a mixed economy in which state
enterprises were expected to recoup expenditures
from revenues.  There was required a separate
accounting for the results of each state
enterprise.
     The adoption in April 1929 of the first five
year plan for national economic development made
urgent the resolution of the question of the
function of accounting in the socialist economy.
There was a sharp difference of view between the
accounting specialists educated prior to the
October Revolution and the Party activists.  The
former group considered that accounting data
generated within the enterprise would be used in
its management and not merely processed for
transmission to a superior level of state economic
administration.  The Party activists considered
such views to be an expression of bourgeois
ideology and inappropriate for application in the
Soviet economy.

With the creation of the all-union system embracing all state enterprises accounting was restricted to the implementation of a control function.

The controversy over the role of accounting seems to have recurred when socialism was extended to the Baltic Republics, Poland and Czechoslovakia (i.e. countries with established accounting traditions) during the late nineteen-forties.

The absence of alternative models of socialist accounting was a major reason for the adoption of the Soviet model in the late nineteen-forties by those European countries embarking upon a path of socialist development.

Brzezin and Jaruga distinguish two periods in the evolution of accounting in European socialist countries:

1945-1956 Widespread adoption of the Soviet model of accounting

1956- Soviet accounting model subjected to modification in a number of socialist countries.

At the Twentieth Congress of the Communist Party of the Soviet Union, held in February 1956, the right of each of the socialist countries to pursue its own path of economic and social development was acknowledged. In subsequent years modifications to the structure of the economic institutions and to the relations between the central authorities and the enterprises were undertaken in a number of socialist countries. These measures of economic reform created a need for a modification to the accounting system. In individual countries the departure from the Soviet model was marked by the introduction of a revised national chart of accounts. For example, in 1960 a new chart of accounts was adopted in Poland. Only in Bulgaria has there continued to be a close adherence to the Soviet accounting model.

Nevertheless there continued to be prominent features common to accounting in the socialist countries. A standardised accounting system is implemented compulsorily in all units of micro-economic activity. The ultimate responsibility for the design, implementation and development of the standardised accounting system is entrusted to a designated central authority. In

the German Democratic Republic the responsibility
is discharged by the Central Board for Statistics
although in the majority of countries the relevant
authority is the Ministry of Finance.

In the preceding chapters the scope of the
standardised accounting system is emphasised. It
embraces:

- national chart of accounts

- accounting records

- accounting terminology

- rules governing the accounting entries

- accounting returns and reports.

For all practical purposes the regulations
governing the operation of the accounting system
form a branch of administrative law.

With the extension of economic reform and the
enlargement of the powers of the executives of the
enterprises there has tended to occur a curtailment
of the detailed prescriptions for accounting
practice previously contained in the regulations
issued by the central authorities. Consequently,
the enterprise has been enabled to modify to some
extent the accounting system so as to meet the
evolving information needs of its own management.
That is, the more centralised is the control of the
national economy so the more detailed are the
accounting regulations issued to the enterprises.

In the command economy initially only the
central authorities (e.g. the controlling
industrial ministries, the ministry of finance, the
state planning authority, the state price fixing
authority, the state bank) are recognised as users
of the accounting data processed by the accounting
systems installed in the enterprises. Only with
the progress of economic reform are the managements
of enterprises recognised as users of accounting
information and measures taken to enable their
needs to be accommodated within the accounting
system.

The familiar features of double entry record,
ledger account and balance sheet are incorporated
into the accounting systems of socialist countries.

Natural resources are not valued in the
accounting records of socialist enterprises. In
accordance with Marxian economic theory only the

expenditure of labour effort is considered to impart value to assets. The means of production (i.e. fixed assets excluding natural resources) are valued at their cost at the time of acquisition (i.e. the authorised state price). Revaluations occur infrequently. An exception to the general rule is provided by Yugoslavia. In that country there is a relatively flexible pricing structure and fixed assets may be revalued upwards to reflect current market values.

Depreciation is usually based on the fixed instalment method and charged into the accounts at centrally determined rates. The central authorities determine the manner of disposal of the portion of the cash flow equivalent to the amount of depreciation charged in the accounts. The greater part of these resources are channelled into an investment bank so that centralised control can be exercised over the pattern of capital investment. The resources initially set aside by the enterprise for the purpose of plant replacement in practice may be used by the investment bank to extend capital investment elsewhere in the economy.

In the capitalist enterprise the amounts set aside as depreciation are merged into the general pool of working capital. That does not happen in the socialist enterprise so that the central authorities are enabled to exercise a strong direct control or, depending upon the degree of economic decentralisation, a strong indirect influence, over its operations.

The accounting records are based on historic cost. The procedures of accrual accounting are employed. In correspondence with the physical flow of production through the enterprise costs are accumulated in the accounting records so as to ascertain the total cost of output. In the Soviet accounting system deliveries to customers are transferred at cost to a holding account and not released as a charge against income until settlement of the account by the customer has been confirmed by the State Bank. In Poland income is recognised in the accounts when the finished products are dispatched to the customer.

In the Soviet Union bank interest is treated as an appropriation of profit whereas in some socialist countries it is regarded as a charge against income.

Thus, among the socialist countries there are differences with respect to income recognition and profit measurement. Jaruga indicates that in

178

Accounting Under Socialism: An Overview

Poland there is an endeavour to separate the
windfall and irregular profits from the overall
profit so as to obtain a measure that reflects the
result of the collective exertions of the personnel
of the enterprise.  In effect, there is an attempt
to identify efficiency profits.

     In the socialist enterprise the accounting
function is confined to retrospective accounting.
Turk emphasises that in the Yugoslav enterprise
both budgeting and the analysis of accounting
data are separated from the accounting function.
The tasks of the accounting department tend to be
similarly restricted in other socialist countries.
     To strengthen the control of the central
authorities over the activities of an enterprise
resources are made available for specific purposes.
Financial resources are recorded in specially
designated accounts and frequently held in special
accounts at the state bank.  These resources are
released by the state bank to the enterprise for
meeting the expenditures authorised.  The balance
sheet is structured so as to show assets marshalled
into groups corresponding to their source of
financing for the benefit of the authorities
overseeing the enterprise's activities.  Turk
indicates that the balance sheet may contain a
considerable amount of detail.
     Jaruga observes that the accounting system
contributes to the functioning of the financial
system of the socialist country.  The accounting
system is used not only to record but also to
verify the financial flows through the economy.
Through the accounting system the enterprise's
adherence to the rules of the financial system may
be observed.
     Apart from the common features of socialist
accounting present in all the countries considered
there may be observed some significant differences.
     Of special interest is the system developed in
the German Democratic Republic.  In socialist
countries there are usually two separate systems
for the accumulation of data for presentation to
the central authorities.  Apart from the accounting
system there is also the system for the processing
of statistical data.  Within the enterprise the
operation of each system is entrusted to a separate
department.  Inevitably there occurs duplication in
the work of data handling undertaken.
     In the GDR there has been developed an
accountancy and statistics information system that
attempts to meet the data needs of both the

enterprise management and the central authorities.

It may be remarked that during 1931-1932 there was an attempt to create a similar system in the USSR. The attempt proved unsuccessful and was soon abandoned.

Reinecke indicates that for the operation of the system in the GDR it has been necessary to specify comprehensively the information requirements of the system's users. Moreover, the requirement for information is revised continually so that the system may be adapted to the users' changing needs.

There is evidence that the accountancy and statistics information system has not proved in practice to be wholly adequate to the task. Firstly, separate systems for the transmission of data from the enterprises to their appropriate industrial ministries have been retained. Secondly, and perhaps more significantly, there has been the development of in-house systems by large industrial enterprises.

In the design of the standardised accounting systems the central authorities are regarded as the primary users of the information to be generated. When there is an expansion of the authority of the executives of the enterprises the authorised accounting system lacks the flexibility for adaptation to the new situation. The consequence is the emergence of informal data processing systems. In the USSR there may be observed in recent times an expansion of somewhat similar systems, such as the operational financial data system. These systems provide data at shorter intervals, in a format more relevant to the needs of local management and more promptly. The informal systems are more responsive to the changing information needs of local management.

The existence of these informal systems provides an indication of the extent to which the authorised accounting system fails to satisfy the needs of the management of the enterprise.

In the socialist countries, although the standarised accounting systems have been developed primarily to serve the needs of the central authorities, there has been no attempt at an integration of micro-accounting and macro-accounting. Brzezin and Jaruga suggest that the charts of accounts in socialist countries were not designed so as to accommodate the requirements of macro-accounting. In Poland the accounting statements are aggregated only for unions of enterprises. In the USSR the accounting statements are aggregated for individual industrial ministries. There is no aggregation of accounting statements at the national level although the accounting system is a source of data for the construction of individual macro-economic variables.

Brzezin and Jaruga suggest that the further development of socialist accounting is a precondition for the realisation of the integration of micro-accounting and macro-accounting.

Initially the socialist countries were characterised by command economies in which there was a high degree of centralised economic decision-making. Instructions on the composition and volume of output were transmitted from the central authorities to the enterprises. Wierzbicki argues that in the command economy there is relatively little demand for accounting information. Neither at the centre nor in the peripheral enterprises is accounting information significant either in the decision-making process or for the evaluation of performance. Non-accounting criteria (e.g. physical measures of the composition and volume of output) are accorded a major role in the management of the economy both at the centre and in the peripheral enterprises.

In the command economy accounting is perceived as being indispensable for exercising control over the activities of enterprises but is not valued highly for the realisation of economic efficiency.

Accounting regresses to book-keeping, the maintenance of clerical accounting records, in the command economy. At the enterprise the accountant becomes transformed into a book-keeper. The development of accounting theory and practice is retarded. There is a denial of adequate resources for investment in accounting equipment and a deterioration in the quality of accounting personnel.

For the evaluation of enterprise performance attention is transferred to physical indicators of the composition and volume of ouptut (e.g. number of tractors, combine harvesters, and so on produced) generated by the statistical services of the enterprise. It is these indicators that are aggregated to the national level.

Brzezin and Jaruga suggest that the relative importance of the two departments in the enterprise producing either statistical or accounting data is linked to the degree of centralisation in the economy.

Wierzbicki emphasises that an expansion of centralised decision-making in the economy leads to a contraction of accounting at the enterprise. There is also a change in the function of accounting. Instead of servicing the needs of enterprise management accounting now services the needs of the central authorities.

In the command economy there has been provided an accounting suited to its own special requirements. Wierzbicki stresses it is the nature of the economic system, through the demand created for information, that determines the nature of the accounting provided.

Changes in the economic system (e.g. a shift from direct to indirect methods of economic management on the part of the central authorities) by altering the demand for information will create a need for a change in the accounting system.

In the socialist countries with the commencement of the transition from the command economy there is a gradual change from direct to indirect methods of influencing enterprise behaviour. Previously the central authorities had relied upon the issue of instructions to direct the activities of enterprises. But now an increasing use is made of economic instruments (e.g. prices, bank interest, taxes) to motivate enterprises.

Nevertheless, the central planners continue to retain control over the direction and pace of economic development:

'The market mechanism is introduced in selected spheres of economic activity where the central planning authority is ready to accept the individual preferences. This solution relieves the planning apparatus ... of the burdensome task of management in vast spheres of detailed decision-making. At the same time it requires fewer information flows than management within the framework of a centralised system.' [10]

For the socialist country the partial decentralisation of economic decision-making may lead in the longer term to a situation in which:

'All the parameters of the financial system ... constitute an instrument of indirect management, which ensures that

partial profit maximisation leads to a
consistent and efficient overall
solution'. [11]

The active use of such economic instruments as
market prices creates a flow of signals that are
deciphered through the accounting system of the
enterprise. In these conditions accounting
acquires the potential to become an important
source of information for the efficient management
of the enterprise in the socialist economy.
Whether the accounting system will be
developed to provide such information to enterprise
management will be dependent upon the extent to
which the central authorities refrain from
intervention in the operation of the market
mechanism. That is, the central authorities do not
override the messages conveyed by market signals.
For example, the central authorities abstain from
the provision of special financial assistance to
inefficient and unprofitable enterprises. Instead,
the central authorities permit the disbandment of
unprofitable enterprises so that resources may be
released for more efficient use elsewhere within
the economy. That is, the performance of
enterprises is evaluated in terms of profitability
and not, as in the command economy, by volume of
output. In other words, the enterprises are
subjected to a hard budget constraint.

If the enterprises are not consistently
orientated to the generation of profits there is a
relaxation in the pressure to use accounting data
in their efficient management. In consequence
there is a slower development of the theory and
practice of accounting.

For accounting specialists in the capitalist
countries that seems to be the principal lesson to
be drawn from the present examination of accounting
in socialist countries. Nevertheless, Brzezin and
Jaruga have provided an interesting challenge: the
modern theory of accounting should have boundaries
sufficiently broad to embrace the practice of
accounting in both capitalist and socialist
countries.

REFERENCES

1. Engels, F., <u>Anti-Duhring</u>, (FLPH, Moscow,
1954) p.411.
2. Op. cit., p.430.

3. Marx, K., <u>Kapital</u>, Vol.II, (FLPH, Moscow, 1957), p.135.
4. Marx, K. and Engels, F., 'Manifesto of the Communist Party' in K. Marx and F. Engels, <u>Selected Works</u>, Vol.11, (FLPH, Moscow, 1953), p.35.
5. Marx, K., <u>Kapital</u>, Vol.111, (FLPH, Moscow, 1959), p.254.
6. Lenin, V.I., <u>Questions of the Socialist Organisation of the Economy</u>, (Progress, Moscow, undated), p.95.
7. Op. cit., p.91.
8. Op. cit., p.71.
9. Loc. cit.
10.. Trzeciakowski, W., <u>Indirect Management in a Centrally Managed Economy</u>, (North Holland, Amsterdam, 1978), p.16.
11. Op. cit., p.14.